The Bedford Glossary
for European History

The Bedford Glossary for European History

Eric F. Johnson

Kutztown State University of Pennsylvania

Andrew J. Donnelly

Loyola University Chicago

Gabriel K. Wolfenstein

University of California, Los Angeles

Bedford/St. Martin's
Boston ◆ New York

For Bedford/St. Martin's

Executive Editor for History: Mary V. Dougherty
Director of Development for History: Jane Knetzger
Developmental Editors: Debra Michals and Shannon Hunt
Production Editor: Katherine Caruana
Projection Supervisor: Andrew Ensor
Senior Marketing Manager: Jenna Bookin Barry
Copyeditor: Lisa Wehrle
Cover Design: Billy Boardman
Composition: DeNee Reiton Skipper
Printing and Binding: Malloy Lithographing, Inc.

President: Joan E. Feinberg
Editorial Director: Denise B. Wydra
Director of Marketing: Karen Melton Soeltz
Director of Edition, Design and Production: Marcia Cohen
Managing Editor: Elizabeth M. Schaaf

Library of Congress Control Number: 2006933434

Manufactured in the United States of America.

1 0 9 8 7
f   e   d   c

For information, write: Bedford/St. Martin's, 75 Arlington Street, Boston, MA 02116
(617-399-4000)

ISBN-10: 0–312–45717–0
ISBN-13: 978–0–312–45717–4

D0033091

Preface

The Bedford Glossary for European History offers students clear, concise definitions of terms they need to know in order to get the most from a European history course. This portable volume contains vocabulary that students will encounter in their reading for the Western Civilization survey as well as in contemporary media, enabling them to participate knowledgeably in discussions inside and outside the classroom. The terms are arranged alphabetically and cover political, economic, social, and cultural topics. Definitions provide a time period and historical context to help students locate the term in European history and comprehend its significance. Incorporating and expanding on the glossaries found in Bedford/St. Martin's Western Civilization survey text—*The Making of the West,* by Lynn Hunt, Thomas R. Martin, Barbara H. Rosenwein, R. Po-chia Hsia, and Bonnie G. Smith—*The Bedford Glossary for European History* serves as a handy supplement for both the complete and concise versions of this book.

The Bedford Glossary
for European History

A

Abbasid The caliphal dynasty that came to power in 750 C.E. in what is now Iran, replacing the Umayyad dynasty and led by caliphs who could trace their authority as religious and secular leaders directly back to the Prophet Muhammad (c. 570–632 C.E.). Questioning the legitimacy of the Umayyads, the Abbasids gained control as rulers of the region through civil war by forging an uneasy coalition of primarily Shi'ites and non-Arabs excluded from the Umayyad government. The Abbasids moved the Islamic capital from its longtime home in Damascus to Baghdad, developed a centralized administration, and exercised considerable power over the Islamic world until the late ninth century. *See also* caliphs.

abolitionists Advocates for the outlawing of the slave trade and the end of slavery. Abolitionist groups and associations began to form in Britain, France, and the United States at the end of the eighteenth century, publishing antislavery newspapers and petitioning governments. Abolitionism drew inspiration from the principles of the Enlightenment, an intellectual movement that began in western Europe in the late seventeenth century that stressed the power of human reason, intellect, and science and supported religious toleration. Some of the first antislavery societies were religious groups such as the Quakers, who prohibited their members from owning slaves.

absolutism A system of government in which a monarch holds sole and uncontestable power over the state and his or her subjects. Absolutist theory linked royal power with divine authority, presenting the monarch as God's lieutenant on earth. It was most prevalent in the seventeenth century and emerged in response to decades of religious warfare, which fueled public demand for a strong ruler who could maintain order. It is best exemplified by Louis XIV (r. 1643–1715) of France. Other absolutist states included Russia, Prussia, and the Austrian Hapsburg Empire. *See also* constitutionalism.

Act of Supremacy Passed by the English Parliament in 1534, the Act of Supremacy completed England's break with the papacy by declaring Henry VIII the head of the Church of England, or Anglican church. It also allowed the monarchy to confiscate church property. *See also* Church of England.

agora The central market square of the Greek city-state and an important feature of Greek life, where people shopped or gathered for conversation. The agora's architecture was designed to facilitate this communal assembly, as wealthy elites voluntarily constructed public buildings to demonstrate their own greatness. For example, the Athenian commander Cimon financed the construction of the Painted Stoa, whose paintings hailed his family, including his father's ship at the battle of Marathon (490 B.C.E.). *See also* city-state; polis.

agricultural revolution Increasingly aggressive attitudes toward investment in and management of farmland in the 1700s that resulted in increased food production. Credited to the British, who adopted and advanced seventeenth-century Dutch and Flemish agricultural innovations, the agricultural revolution was marked by an expansion in the amount of cultivated land; the consolidation of small, scattered plots into larger, more efficient farms; new strategies that linked livestock raising with crop cultivation to replenish minerals in the soil; and the selective breeding of animals to increase a herd's population, size, and health. Although the food output increased more than 40 percent over the course of the century and food prices dropped accordingly, the agricultural revolution put added pressure on small farmers and rural villagers.

aids Payments made by a vassal to his lord on important occasions, such as the knighting of the lord's eldest son or the marriage of his eldest daughter. Aids were part of the system of obligations by which a vassal was bound to a ruler. King William I of England (r. 1066–1087 C.E.), for example, required the payment of aids in return for his gifts of fiefs throughout England. *See also* vassalage.

Albigensians The name given by its opponents to a religious movement centered in Albi in southern France in the twelfth century. Albigensians espoused a form of dualism and renounced the perceived evils of the world, including wealth, meat, and sex. They were labeled as heretics by the church, and a crusade was launched against them between 1209 and 1229.

Almohades An Islamic people from North Africa who invaded the Muslim-controlled portion of Spain in the 1170s. Muslim disunity in the Iberian peninsula was exacerbated by this invasion and the Almohades's strict belief in religious purity, thereby producing conditions favorable for the Christian reconquest of 1212.

Anabaptists A religious sect started in Zurich, Switzerland, in the sixteenth century that believed that true faith was based on reason and free will and that people must knowingly select the Christian faith through rebaptism as adults. These men and women rejected the authority of the state and the courts, abolished private property, and believed themselves to be true Christians who lived according to the standards established in the Bible. The movement gained most of its support from artisans and the middle and lower classes, who were attracted by its simple message of peace and salvation. Anabaptists were persecuted by both Catholic and Protestant authorities, and Zurich's magistrates, angered at the pacifist sect's refusal to bear arms, ordered that hundreds of Anabaptists be put to death, thereby making them the Reformation's first martyrs of conscience. Nonetheless, Anabaptism spread first to Germany and then throughout northwestern Europe.

anarchism The belief that government is unnecessary and undesirable and should be replaced with voluntary cooperation and free association. As a political movement, it emerged in the nineteenth century and was popular among peasants and workers who felt oppressed by their governments and large landowners. Anarchism was embraced by early labor unions, especially after they were outlawed in Russia and across Europe after 1850. Anarchists actively sought the creation of a stateless society and advocated extreme tactics, including violence and murder, to overthrow the government. In the 1880s, anarchists bombed businesses and government offices; in the 1890s, they assassinated leaders such as Spanish premier Antonio Canvas del Castillo (1897), Empress Elizabeth of Austria-Hungary (1898), King Umberto of Italy (1900), and U.S. president William McKinley (1900).

Angevin The ruling dynasty of England that originated in the French county of Anjou. The Angevins, also called Plantagenets by historians, came to power with the accession to the throne of King Henry II (r. 1154–1189). With Henry's marriage to Eleanor of Aquitaine in 1152, the Angevins gained control of large areas of France. The two nations would struggle over that land throughout Angevin rule. *See also* Plantagenet.

Anglican church *See* Church of England.

Anglo-Saxon England A term referring to England after the invasions of the Angles and Saxons (beginning in the 440s C.E.) and before the Norman conquest in 1066. Christianity was introduced to northern Anglo-Saxon England in the fifth century by Irish monks and in the south by papal missionaries in 597.

Anschluss   German for "union"; the desire for the unification of the German-speaking lands of Austria and Germany. The union took place when Hitler annexed Austria in 1938.

anti-Semitism   Prejudice against Jews. Its history dates back to the Middle Ages, when discrimination against Jews was primarily religious and resulted in exile or economic, personal, and political restrictions. After the eighteenth-century Enlightenment lifted these limits, anti-Jewish bias arose in their place, and by the nineteenth and twentieth centuries, anti-Semitism became a significant component of social and political movements. Anti-Semites, particularly in Germany and Austria-Hungary but other Western countries as well, held that Jews were an inferior race, were responsible for the problems of modern society, and had been the main beneficiaries of economic change and strife. These beliefs served as the basis for the Holocaust during World War II, in which Adolf Hitler exterminated approximately six million European Jews between 1939 and 1945.

apartheid   A South African policy of racial segregation and political and economic discrimination against nonwhites instituted to ensure a white-dominated society. Though segregation was widespread prior to the middle of the twentieth century, it was not until the National Party came to power in 1948 that it was formally named and adopted. Opposition from the United Nations and other groups and individuals worldwide gathered momentum beginning in the 1960s, but the most meaningful antiapartheid efforts were economic—among them, divestiture of U.S. and other corporate interests in the region and U.S. insistence that its firms there hire workers without discrimination. Apartheid laws were repealed in 1991.

apocalypticism   The belief in a period of great crisis, followed by the end of the earthly world, judgment, and salvation. Meaning the "uncovering of the future," apocalypticism was an aspect of Hebrew monotheism (consolidated 1000–539 B.C.E.) that came to influence the development of Christianity. *See also* monotheism.

apostate   Latin for "renegade from the faith"; one who rejects his or her original religion. The Roman emperor Julian (r. 361–363 C.E.) was known as "the Apostate" for abandoning Christianity and spreading his own philosophical brand of paganism.

apostolic succession   The principle by which Christian bishops upheld their authority and declared their right to appoint their successors. The doctrine of apostolic succession states that all bishops could trace their authority back to the Apostles of Jesus, who granted their successors the same authority that Jesus (c. 4 B.C.E.–30 C.E.) had given to them. Bishops could ordain priests with the power to administer the sacraments and control their congregation's membership and finances.

appeasement The strategy of preventing war by making concessions for seemingly legitimate grievances. Although British and French leaders believed that using an appeasement strategy with Nazi Germany in the 1930s would secure "peace in our time," they were ultimately wrong. The Munich Pact of 1938 attempted to prevent large-scale war by granting German chancellor Adolf Hitler his demand for control over the Sudeten-land, a German-populated region bordering Czechoslovakia. Instead, it verified Hitler's theory that the West would not inter-fere in eastern Europe, gave him time to build an army, and emboldened him to continue the invasions—beginning with Czechoslovakia just months later—that led to World War II (1939–1945).

aretê Greek for "excellence." In Dark Age Greece (c. 1000–750 B.C.E.), aretê signified the high social value placed on com-petition and outdoing others as a means of increasing one's own social standing. Such ideals were evident in the deeds of the elite heroes in Homer's *The Iliad* and *The Odyssey*. *See also* Dark Age.

Arianism Christian doctrine named for its founder, Arius (c. 260–336 C.E.), that maintained that God created Jesus from nothing and then bestowed him with special status. Therefore, Jesus was not co-eternal or identical in nature with God. Ari-anism was immensely popular but problematic for those who believed in the unity of the Holy Trinity—Father, Son, and Holy Ghost. The issue was resolved when the Council of Nicaea voted to condemn Arianism as heresy in 325 C.E. Although Arius was banished, his missionaries later converted many non-Romans who poured into the empire.

art nouveau A late-nineteenth-century style in the arts, house-hold and fashion design, and graphics that featured flowing lines, intertwined vines and flowers, and curvaceous female forms. Part of the modern art movement in western Europe, it arose in direct contrast to the historical realism of mid-nineteenth-century art. Borrowing from Asian and African motifs, designers used natural elements to offset the mechanized and cold reality of factory and office work, seeking to create beautiful things for the general public in everything from dishes to coins to street lamps and buildings. Commercially successful and instantly popular with both the government and the masses, art nouveau was the exception to public distaste for innovations in the visual arts.

asceticism From the Greek for "training"; the practice of physical self-denial. St. Augustine (354–430 C.E.) emphasized the centrality of asceticism, especially sexual abstinence, to Christianity; it later became an important religious tenet, especially for monks and priests.

atheist A person who does not believe in the existence of God. Atheism became prominent in the West during the Enlightenment of the eighteenth century, as scientists and philosophers discovered natural explanations for how the universe operated that did not rely on divine intervention. *See also* deist; Enlightenment.

Atlantic revolutions A series of protest movements demanding greater liberty that appeared on both sides of the Atlantic Ocean in the late 1780s and early 1790s, including and at times inspired by both the American Revolution (1775–1783) and the French Revolution (1792–1801). The Atlantic revolutions were the product of growing prosperity and high expectations among the increasingly wealthy and educated. The French Revolution was the most violent, long-lasting, and ultimately influential of those in western Europe. It inspired slaves in the French Caribbean colony of St. Domingue to revolt against their masters in 1791 and win independence as the country of Haiti in 1804.

Atlantic system The triangular pattern of trade established in the 1700s that bound together western Europe, Africa, and the Americas. Europeans traded goods to purchase slaves from western Africa and sold them in the Americas, where their labor produced commodities such as coffee and sugar that were then sold at European ports for refinement or reshipment. The Atlantic system also provided new markets for items manufactured in Europe, often using raw materials produced on plantations in the Americas.

atonality A musical style initiated by Austrian composer Arnold Schoenberg (1874–1951) in the early twentieth century, which sought the removal of any melodic reference to tonal centers, or keys. It ultimately led to the emergence of a twelve-tone scale.

auctoritas Latin for "moral authority"; a prized Roman virtue. Roman ruler Augustus (r. 27 B.C.E.–14 C.E.) transformed the power structure of the republic by claiming the title of princeps or "first man" for himself, alleging to rule by auctoritas rather than sheer political or military might. In truth, he controlled both the state and its troops, ultimately making the military the foundation for his moral authority by turning the republic's citizen militia into a professional force.

auto da fé Portuguese for "demonstration" or "act of faith"; a ritual of public confession and humiliation for heretics and those suspected of heresy in Spain and Portugal during the Inquisition. Imposed and overseen by the Catholic church, the first auto da fé took place in Seville, Spain, in 1481, and the practice continued into the nineteenth century. *See also* heresy; Inquisition.

B

ban Social, economic, and political rights originally held by medieval royalty. By 1000, however, the right to collect taxes, hear court cases, levy fines, and muster men for defense via the ban had been assumed by increasingly powerful local landlords at the expense of monarchs.

baroque An artistic style that emerged in Rome in the seventeenth century and flourished in the Catholic Hapsburg territories of Spain. Featuring curves, exaggerated lighting, intense emotions, release from restraint, and even a kind of artistic sensationalism, the baroque style departed from the Renaissance emphasis on harmonious and precise design. Baroque art was closely tied to the Catholic Reformation and often used religious themes to reaffirm the emotional depths of the Catholic faith and to glorify both the church and the monarchy. *See also* classicism.

battle of Britain Also known as the Blitz, the 1940 air assault on Britain by Nazi Germany's Luftwaffe (air force) during World War II (1939–1945). Although it wreaked much destruction on monuments and buildings in London and other industrial cities, the invasion also intensified Britain's research and development of antiaircraft weapons, its highly successful code-detecting group Ultra, and its advances in radar. By year's end, the British air industry was outproducing the Germans by 50 percent.

battle of Stalingrad The 1942 assault on the Russian city of Stalingrad by German forces during World War II (1939–1945). Seen as an opportunity by Germany to gain access to Soviet oil, the siege was ultimately a major miscalculation. After months of expensive and violent fighting, Germany was defeated, and ninety thousand surviving soldiers were captured. The battle represented a turning point in the war on the Eastern front, as Russia continued to push West against Nazi forces on the ground.

battle of the Somme A 1916 World War I (1914–1918) battle between German and British forces, fought along the Somme River in France. Ending in a stalemate, the bitter three-month conflict is notable for the high number of casualties—1.25 million men killed or wounded—and the first use of tanks in warfare.

Beguines Laywomen in northern Europe who elected to live together in informal pious communities at the end of the twelfth century. They embraced celibacy and often made their living by weaving cloth or working with the sick and old. Their spiritual lives were often emotional and ecstatic, infused with imagery of love and religion.

Benedictines The monastic order founded in western Europe by Benedict of Nursia (c. 480–553 C.E.) that was strongly influential on Catholic worship. Benedict's code (c. 540 C.E.), which outlined his monastery's daily prayer routine, scriptural readings, and manual labor, did not isolate monks from the outside world nor deprive them of sleep, food, or warm clothing, as did other monastic orders.

benefices A system of ecclesiastical, or church, offices, supported by an endowment. In essence, benefices are stipends paid to clergy in exchange for performing religious duties such as holding mass. Early benefices, particularly in medieval times, were in the form of land grants. Some benefices were quite substantial and allowed their holders to live in great comfort, although by definition, clergy were supposed to dedicate any excess toward good works. The holding of vast and multiple benefices led to abuse and secular and religious conflicts.

beneficia Latin for "benefits" or "fiefs"; landed estates that were often given by a lord to his vassal in exchange for service. The vassal could continue to use the land as long as he maintained his loyalty and obligation to the lord. The giving of beneficia by Pope Hadrian IV (r. 1154–1159) in 1157 to Emperor Frederick I Barbarossa (r. 1152–1190) was seen by many as an attempt by the pope to make Frederick his vassal. *See also* vassalage.

Berlin airlift Efforts, primarily by the United States, to fly in millions of tons of food and heating fuel to over two million isolated residents of West Berlin in 1948–1949. In an attempt to force Allied nations out of Berlin, the Soviets blockaded all access to the city, which had been partitioned between Western powers and the Soviet Union at the end of World War II (1939–1945). The United States made daily deliveries until the Soviets finally lifted the blockade. This incident led to the division of Germany into the Federal Republic of Germany in the west and the German Democratic Republic in the east.

Berlin Wall A twenty-eight mile wall built by the Soviet Union in 1961 along the border of East and West Berlin to prevent East Germans from leaving for the West. Initially barbed wire, it was soon replaced by a concrete wall topped with barbed wire and gradually extended beyond the two cities to encompass the entire boundary between East and West Germany. It became emblematic of the cold war and kept Germany separated until the Soviets agreed to remove it in 1989, in part as a gesture they hoped would keep the faltering Communist Party in power.

The "Big Three" The leaders of the three major Allied nations during and after World War II (1939–1945): the U.S. president Franklin Delano Roosevelt (1933–1945), the British prime minister Winston Churchill (1940–1945), and the Soviet Union's premier Joseph Stalin (1924–1953). The term referred to the meetings held by these leaders to discuss the running of the war and postwar concerns such as the demarcation of boundaries. Harry S. Truman (1945–1953) took over for the United States after Roosevelt's death, and Clement Attlee (1945–1951) represented Britain following the victory of the Labour Party in 1945.

birth control Broadly speaking, efforts to determine and limit family size through techniques that block conception. Contraceptives date back to ancient times, but the vulcanization of rubber in the 1840s made possible the widespread production and sale of more reliable condoms. As birth control became increasingly popular, some religious leaders labeled it immoral; other critics claimed middle-class birth control users harmed national welfare by putting fewer "quality" children into society. Access to and development of better birth control methods inspired the birth control movement worldwide. In the twentieth century, the invention of the contraceptive pill in 1960 has been linked to women's liberation and increasing public discussions of sexuality.

Black Death An epidemic that originated in Asia, arrived in Europe in 1347, and reappeared intermittently until the early eighteenth century. Traditionally thought to be bubonic plague, the first outbreak killed at least one-third of the population of Europe and was one of several catastrophes in the fourteenth century that shook the foundations of medieval society and created a climate of fear. Many believed the disease was God's way of punishing sinners, and some sought to save themselves by traveling in bands throughout Germany and the Roman Empire, whipping themselves in penance. The visits of these flagellants sometimes sparked violence against Jews, whom many blamed for the sickness. Although socially and economically devastating, the Black Death also created new economic opportunities for survivors by reducing competition for land and resources, previously strained by rapid population growth. *See also* flagellants.

black power A movement and a philosophical approach to gaining civil and political rights for African Americans in the 1960s. Associated with black nationalism, the black power sociopolitical movement actively encouraged a separate identity and a sense of pride for people of African heritage. Some advocated for black power leaders to demand rights, even through violence if necessary, rather than beg for them through nonviolent protests or demonstrations.

Blitzkrieg German for "lightning war"; a strategy for the conduct of war in which motorized firepower quickly and overwhelmingly attacks the enemy, leaving it unable to resist militarily or psychologically. It was first used on a large scale by the German army in World War II (1939–1945). *See also* battle of Britain.

Boer War The war between Britain and Boer (Dutch-descended) inhabitants of South Africa for control of the region, which lasted from 1899 to 1902. Although it played on British imperialist fervor, the war's heavy casualties and bloodshed, as well as the unfit conditions of British soldiers and inhumane treatment of South Africans, subsequently convinced many Britons that empire was morally wrong—for some, in fact, imperialism was equal to barbarism—or at least too costly to maintain. Britain ultimately annexed the area in 1902, but the cost in money, destruction, and human life was enormous.

Bolshevik From the Russian for "majority," V. I. Lenin's (1840–1924) faction of the Social Democratic Party in Russia, which seized power in October 1917. Unlike most Marxists, who stressed the power of laboring people, Lenin stressed that a highly disciplined socialist elite—rather than the working class as a whole—would lead Russia to socialism. The Bolsheviks, often in the minority during their early history, later became the Communist Party in Russia.

Bolshevik Revolution The overthrow of Russia's Provisional Government in the fall of 1917 by V. I. Lenin (1870–1924) and his Bolshevik forces, made possible by the government's continuing defeat in the war, its failure to bring political reform, and a further decline in the conditions of everyday life.

Boxer Rebellion An attempt to remove all outsiders from China in 1900. Uprisings began after the defeat by Japan five years earlier forced the ruling Qing dynasty to grant more economic concessions to Western powers. In response, peasants formed secret societies to restore Chinese integrity; one was known as the Society of the Righteous and Harmonious Fists, or Boxers, so named because members believed that ritual boxing would protect them from social and other evils. Missionaries and Chinese Christians, whom the peasants partly blamed for China's troubles, were massacred during the rebellion. After the revolt was put down, harsh terms, including significant foreign control, were imposed.

Bronze Age Considered the earliest era of civilization (c. 4000–1000 B.C.E.). The name denotes the widespread use of bronze, an alloy of copper and tin, in tools and weaponry. In Europe and the Near East, the Bronze Age was marked by increasing divides between wealthy and poor and men and women. Bronze Age civilizations became gradually complex, as long-distance commerce developed and rulers created legal systems to promote justice and solidify their own power.

buccaneers Bands of pirates who formed in the late 1600s and concentrated their activities in the Caribbean region. Buccaneers were primarily made up of English, French, and Dutch deserters and the crews of wrecked government-sponsored pirate vessels. They governed themselves and preyed on ships regardless of national origin. The word comes from their custom of curing strips of beef, called *boucan* by the native Caribs.

bull An official papal letter or document, named for the bulla or raised seal used to signify its authenticity. Among the more famous bulls were Exsurge Domine (1520), issued by Pope Leo X (r. 1513–1521) against Martin Luther (1483–1546), and Pastor aeternus (1871), issued by Pope Pius IX (r. 1846–1878) on papal infallibility.

bureaucracy A hierarchical system of organization in business and government in which authority is distributed among individuals and departments according to specialization. These units are connected and overseen by a central governing body. The development of bureaucracies in the seventeenth century was an essential component in the centralization of state authority in early modern governments because they represented the interests of the state against entrenched local interests, such as provincial estates and the nobility. *See also* census.

Byzantine Empire The eastern Roman Empire, centered in Byzantium, which Emperor Constantine I (r. 306–337 C.E.) reconstructed as Constantinople in 325. By about 500, the empire had achieved vast wealth. Byzantine emperors ruled in the capital of Constantinople until 1453, when a Turkish army captured the city.

C

caballeros villanos Spanish for "city horsemen"; leaders of Spanish towns who were wealthy enough to fight on horseback and came to monopolize municipal political offices. When Alfonso IX (r. 1188–1230) summoned town leaders to his royal court for the first time in 1188, the caballeros served as their representatives, joining the bishops and noblemen in formally counseling the king.

caliphs Successors of the Prophet Muhammad (c. 570–632 C.E.) following his death. Both religious and secular leaders, caliphs were originally selected from Muhammad's inner circle. Disputes over the legitimacy of the succession of caliphs Uthman (644–656 C.E.) and Ali (656–661 C.E.) led to the schism between Sunni and Shi'ite Muslims that continues today. *See also* Abbasid.

canon law The law of the Roman Catholic church. Originally a loose collection of papal decrees and edicts from church councils about the rules and practice of the faith, canon law became a means through which the papacy asserted its authority over the church and medieval society. Pope Leo IX (r. 1049–1054) was one of the first popes to use canon law to justify claims for papal supremacy. Around 1140, a legal scholar named Gratian composed a synthesis of canon law and papal decrees called the *Decretum,* which was one of the foundations of the so-called papal monarchy of the Middle Ages.

canton system A system instituted in Prussia by Frederick William I (r. 1713–1740) in 1733 to create a reserve army and expand Prussia's military capacity. Youths in each canton (district) were given two or three months of army training annually; they could then return to their homes for the rest of the year, where they would remain in reserve for as long as they were able-bodied. Despite its small general population, this system gave Prussia one of the largest armies in Europe.

Capetian A family dynasty that rose to control the French crown from 987 until the fourteenth century. The Capetians, who came to power as the Carolingian dynasty faded, elected the prestigious lord Hugh Capet to the throne. Capetian kings were anointed with holy oil and represented the idea of unity. While the Capetian kings were highly regarded, they controlled only small areas of France and therefore wielded very little power.

capital-intensive industry A mid- to late-nineteenth-century development in which businesses increased profits by investing large sums of money in machinery and infrastructure instead of merely hiring more workers. Common in manufacturing, it contrasts with labor-intensive industry, in which the greatest expenses are for workers. *See also* labor-intensive industry.

capitalism An economic system in which the means of production—labor, machines, and financial investment—are controlled by private individuals or institutions for their own personal profit. Modern capitalism is based on Adam Smith's 1776 work, *The Wealth of Nations*, and takes as its central tenet a belief in free enterprise—that is, that market forces of supply and demand, not government intervention, should be the determining factors in the economy.

carbonari A network of secret societies in Italy that developed in the early nineteenth century to resist Napoleonic rule. Named after the charcoal mark inscribed on the foreheads of new members, the carbonari played an important role in the development of Italian nationalism throughout the nineteenth century and were instrumental in Italian unification.

caricature A style of cartoon, often political in nature, in which the person or persons represented are humorously distorted for the purpose of satire or derision.

Caroline minuscule The clear and beautiful letter forms of the Carolingian era. Caroline minuscule was invented in the ninth century to standardize handwriting so texts would be readable across Charlemagne's (r. 768–814 C.E.) empire.

Carolingian renaissance The revival of learning inaugurated during the rule of Charlemagne (r. 768–814 C.E.). Its objective was to enhance the glory of the kings, educate their officials, reform the liturgy, and purify the faith. Emphasis was placed on resuscitating the learning of the past, particularly that of the Romans. The Carolingian renaissance outlasted the Carolingian dynasty and served as a model for the development of monastic schools and the revival of learning that occurred in the twelfth century.

Carthusians The monastic order founded by Bruno of Cologne (c. 1030–1101) at the end of the eleventh century. A Carthusian monk took a vow of silence and lived as a hermit in his own small hut, only occasionally joining fellow monks for common prayer. Carthusian monks spent most of their time copying manuscripts, a duty they considered a religious vocation. With each monastery limited to twelve monks, the Carthusian order grew slowly.

castellan A person who controlled a castle, the key to power for local lords. As the authority of the king of France waned after the year 1000, castellans increasingly acted as virtual rulers of the small territories around them.

Catholic Reformation (Counter-Reformation) The sixteenth-century religious movement that arose within the Roman Catholic church to preserve and improve the church in response to the critiques of the Protestant Reformation. Like their Protestant counterparts, Catholic reformers sought to address corruption within the church. But unlike Protestants, these reformers wanted to preserve Catholic theology and traditions. New religious orders, such as the Capuchins and the Ursulines, were founded to focus on specific goals and strategies for reform. The Society of Jesus (the Jesuits) stressed that through disciplined and meditative study, individuals could control their emotions and their behavior and ultimately submit to the church and its teachings. This powerful message helped return many Protestants to Catholicism. The church then reasserted its doctrine at the Council of Trent, held intermittently from 1545 to 1563, where reforms were established to end the sale of church offices and strengthen church structure. *See also* Protestants; Reformation.

census The collection of data about the population of a specific region, town, or nation as a whole. The information gathered includes age, race, occupation, marital status, family size, and other data about residents that can be used to develop policies, determine political apportionment, and evenly distribute resources. Essential to the functioning of the state, modern censuses began at the turn of the nineteenth century with the rise of modern bureaucracies. *See also* bureaucracy.

chansons de geste Long narrative poems popular in the eleventh century written in the vernacular, or the language spoken by people in secular society, that celebrated knightly and heroic deeds.

Chartism The movement of supporters of the People's Charter (drawn up in Britain in 1838), which sought to transform Britain into a democracy and demanded universal suffrage for men, vote by secret ballot, equal electoral districts, annual elections, and the elimination of property qualifications for and the payment of stipends to members of Parliament. Chartism attracted many working-class adherents, as well as women, who founded political unions, set up Chartist Sunday schools, organized boycotts of unsympathetic shopkeepers, and joined Chartist temperance associations. Although Chartists galvanized powerful early support, including collecting a million signatures for a petition, their impact waned after 1848.

Chernobyl A now-abandoned city where a reactor exploded in a nuclear power plant on April 26, 1986. It was the worst accident in nuclear power plant history, with over eight thousand deaths and forty thousand people evacuated. Many area residents later developed thyroid cancer, birth defects, and other ailments as a result. The Communist government denied the accident and attempted to cover it up, until Swedish scientists identified the fallout. The delays had dire consequences for those affected by the catastrophe and inspired widespread public questioning of the Communist Party's leaders and policies.

chivalry From the French *cheval*, for "horse"; the ideal, proper code of comportment for a knight. Chivalrous knights as depicted in twelfth- and thirteenth-century literature were gentle in life, valorous in battle, and constrained by a code of refinement, fair play, piety, and devotion to this ideal. How closely real knights lived up to the code of chivalry is debatable; however, they regarded it as an ideal and an objective.

cholera An epidemic, usually fatal disease that appeared in the 1830s in Europe and Asia, reaching the United States in 1849–1850. It was caused by a waterborne bacterium that induced violent vomiting and diarrhea and left the skin blue, eyes sunken and dull, and hands and feet ice cold. Advances in sanitation led to its decline toward the end of the nineteenth century.

Christ From the Greek for "anointed one"; a central figure in apocalyptic religious ideology. Christian and Jewish beliefs held that a Messiah, or Christ, would be sent by God to Earth to conquer evil and bring about a final judgment that would reward the good and punish the bad. According to the Jews, this event has not yet happened. According to Christians, Jesus of Nazareth (c. 4 B.C.E.–30 C.E.) was Christ.

Christian Democrats Powerful center to center-right political parties that evolved in the late 1940s in Europe from former Catholic parties of the pre–World War II period. Christian parties gained increasing support in the postwar era, winning elections in part because of their participation in wartime resistance. A vital component of postwar politics, these groups shifted from their decades-old emphasis on advocating church interests to welcoming non-Catholics among their ranks and focusing on democracy, anticommunism, and social reform.

Christian humanists Intellectuals in the late fifteenth and early sixteenth centuries who dreamed of idealistic societies based on peace, morality, and Christian virtue and sought to realize the ethical ideals of the classical world and the Scriptures. Their ideals applied the techniques and outlook of renaissance humanism to Christianity and the Bible and strongly influenced Martin Luther (1483–1546) and other early Protestant reformers, such as Desiderius Erasmus (c. 1466–1536) and Thomas More (1478–1535). *See also* Reformation.

Church of England Protestant church—and the official church of England—created by Henry VII (r. 1509–1547) in 1534 to supplant the Roman Catholic church. Although initially opposed to Protestantism—even executing some of its leaders—Henry changed his mind when the pope refused to approve his divorce in 1527. In response, he appointed two Protestants to high posts: Thomas Cromwell (1485–1540) as chancellor and Thomas Cranmer (1489–1556) as archbishop of Canterbury. Henry instructed Parliament to outlaw the Catholic church and declare him "the only supreme head of the Church of England." Cromwell and Cranmer pushed Parliament to pass a number of measures from 1527 to 1536 that permanently severed the English church's ties to Rome. Henry, however, found himself at odds with both Catholics, who wanted to return the Church of England to the pope, and Protestants (Puritans), who wanted to further reform the church. After much waxing and waning under Henry's successors, Protestantism won out in England—but never to the Puritans' liking. Many Puritans departed for America in the seventeenth and eighteenth centuries to found communities devoted to their religious ideals. *See also* Act of Supremacy; Protestants.

cinématographe The motion picture, or movie, invented by French brothers Auguste and Louis Lumière in the late nineteenth century. An improvement on Thomas Edison's earlier kinescope, it quickly became an important leisure activity for the general public. In addition to representing popular culture, it was also used as a political tool for propaganda.

Ciompi uprising An urban revolt of the poor in Florence, Italy, in 1378. The ciompi were woolworkers who faced high unemployment due to a slump in the textile industry partly caused by the Black Death, a plague that ravaged the masses. Joined by artisans and merchants, the ciompi demanded more equitable power sharing with the bankers, wealthy merchants, and other urban elites who controlled city government. Crowds thronged the streets, setting fire to the palaces and demanding the right to form their own guilds. As the revolt became too radical, artisan guilds withdrew their support. The patrician regime was restored, although urban unrest, particularly among workers, continued throughout the 1380s. *See also* Black Death.

Cistercians A monastic order founded in 1098 in Citeaux, France, that emphasized a life of simplicity. Widely popular and respected, Cistercians embraced purity, preferring small standardized churches and white, undyed robes. The most influential Cistercian was St. Bernard of Clairvaux (c. 1090–1153), who preached about Christ's humanity.

city-state A state consisting of an urban center that exercises political and economic control over the countryside around it. Mesopotamian city-states, which first appeared circa 3000 B.C.E., were marked by their strong fortification walls and large temples. The governments of these early city-states effectively organized and managed the labor used to maintain the increasingly complex irrigation systems around the Tigris and Euphrates rivers.

Civil Code The French legal code formulated by Napoleon I (r. 1804–1814) in 1804. Also called the Napoleonic Code, it reaffirmed many of the social liberties that had been introduced during the Revolution (1789–1799) while at the same time reestablishing a patriarchal system. The Civil Code assured property rights, religious liberty, and equal treatment under the law to all classes of men. However, it curtailed many of the rights of women, restricting them to the private sphere of the home and giving males greater authority over them. The Civil Code was imitated in many European countries and in Latin America.

Civil Constitution of the Clergy A body of legislation passed in July 1790 that redefined the relationship between the clergy and the state in France. It allowed for the confiscation of church property formerly used to support the clergy, replacing it with a guarantee of state salaries for clergymen instead. It also stipulated that parish priests and bishops be elected just like public officials. The Civil Constitution, and the National Assembly's attempts to enforce it by requiring the clergy to take an oath, divided public opinion of the French Revolution (1789–1799) and galvanized religious opposition.

civil disobedience Deliberately but peacefully breaking the law to demonstrate its inherent problems and the need for change. Initially used by Mohandas Gandhi (1869–1948) in India in the 1930s and earlier by British suffragists to protest oppression and obtain political change, civil disobedience was adopted by Martin Luther King Jr. (1929–1968) and other civil rights activists in the United States in the 1960s.

civil service Government positions or jobs that are not judicial, legislative, nor military, for which hiring is based on competency measured by a formal exam. Civil service placement dates back to ancient China, though it was not until the nineteenth century that both Europe and the United States began to base government hiring and advancement on merit and training rather than on political connections or family lineage. Government accountants, postal employees, and transportation workers are examples of civil service workers.

civilization A way of life that includes political states based on cities with dense populations, large public buildings, diverse economies, a sense of local identity, and some knowledge of writing. Traditionally, civilization in the West began in Mesopotamia (c. 3000 B.C.E.) and Egypt (c. 3050 B.C.E.) and later spread to Anatolia, then Levant, Crete, and Greece.

classicism A style of painting and architecture that reflects the ideals of the art of antiquity: geometric shapes, order, and harmony of lines took precedence over the sensuous, exuberant, and emotional forms of the baroque. Classicism emerged in seventeenth-century France, where it developed into a French national style distinct from the baroque associated with France's enemies, the Austrian and Spanish Hapsburgs. *See also* baroque.

Cluniac reform A movement started by influential Benedictine monks at the monastery of Cluny in France in the tenth century to reform the church and free it from worldly influences. Established in 910 C.E., Cluny was a prestigious monastery where monks prayed with devotion in ways that sought to guarantee the salvation of all Christians. The abbots of Cluny ultimately decided that the world also needed reform and, by the eleventh century, began to link their program of internal monastic and external worldly reform to the papacy.

Code Noir Laws governing slavery in French colonies issued by Louis XIV (r. 1643–1715) in 1685. Often harsh, the code defined enslavement based on the status of the mother and provided strict outlines for the work habits and religious comportment of slaves and slave owners—for instance, only Roman Catholics could own slaves, slaves could not work on Sundays, own weapons, or hold meetings, and killing one's slave was illegal. In practice, however, many colonial planters ignored these laws, especially those that ensured the slaves' well-being.

codex A book with bound pages. Until the invention of the codex, literature had been preserved primarily on scrolls. Codices, which were less susceptible to damage from rolling and unrolling and easier to read than scrolls, became the standard form of book production in the Byzantine world (post fourth century C.E.) and eventually the rest of Europe. The codex was preferred by early Christian writers and compilers of law code; for example, Justinian's law code, or *Codex* of 534, is so named because it was recorded in this new medium.

cold war The rivalry between the United States and the Soviet Union following World War II that led to massive growth in nuclear weapons on both sides. With both countries vying for dominance, the cold war divided the West and caused acute anxiety in political circles and among the general population. It was a significant force in defining global political and economic relationships through the 1980s.

coloni Roman tenant farmers bound by law under Emperor Diocletian (r. 284–305 C.E.) to the land they worked. Coloni children were also required to farm the same land in an effort to stabilize agricultural production. *See also* Dominate.

colonialism The policy of European imperial expansion prior to the nineteenth century under which larger nations seized and controlled smaller nations, deeming them legal and political dependent.

Colosseum A giant amphitheater in the heart of Rome used for gladiatorial shows and other spectacles. The Colosseum was built during the reign of the Flavian emperor Vespasian (r. 69–79 C.E.) over the remains of Nero's (r. 54–68 C.E.) palace, Domus Aurea.

Colossus An early computer built by British Intelligence's Ultra Project in 1943 with the specific goal of cracking the German Enigma code during World War II (1939–1945). In a few hours, Colossus could decipher code that would have taken humans weeks, providing the Allies with vital information as they prepared for the D-Day invasion. Several technicians who worked on Colossus played a significant role in the development of general-purpose computers in Britain, even though the details of the Colossus itself were kept a secret until the 1970s.

COMECON *See* Council for Mutual Economic Assistance.

Comintern An association of Communist parties founded in 1919 by Russian Bolshevik leader V. I. Lenin (1870–1924), former journalist and devout socialist activist, to promote the spread of the revolution and the preaching of communist principles throughout Europe. It evolved from several groups, among them the Second International Workingmen's Association and the Third International Comintern (short for Communist International). Lenin insisted that all parties submit to the Comintern's twenty-one points of doctrine, including dominance by Moscow, which ultimately caused fragmentation of the groups. *See also* Bolshevik.

commercial revolution A term used by historians to describe the collective effect of the development of a profit-based economy, growth of cities, increased trade, and rise of powerful groups of merchants and artisans in the Middle Ages. The meshing of these forces and trends at the end of the eleventh century prompted the rise of long-distance trade networks, new business arrangements, and greater agricultural production. The commercial revolution spawned the development of important institutions such as corporations, banks, and accounting systems.

Committee of Public Safety An administrative body created by the French National Convention in April 1793 to supervise food distribution, direct the war effort, and detect and punish counterrevolutionaries. With Maximilien Robespierre (1758–1794) at its head, the Committee of Public Safety became the political organ of the Terror, overseeing the prosecution and execution of tens of thousands of French men and women who opposed its policies. *See also* Terror.

common law The law of all England or, more generally, a legal code applying to all members of a state. Its first chief architect was King Henry II (r. 1156–1189), who created a system of traveling royal justices whose authority over certain crimes superseded that of local magistrates. Justices also listened to civil cases and opened up new possibilities for property litigation under royal supervision.

commune Sworn associations of citizens who formed a corporate legal body to govern their town independently of any monarch or lord. First appearing in the early twelfth century, communes became the normal institution of self-government in medieval towns, complete with their own courts of law.

communism A political and economic system in which the state owns all property and citizens ostensibly share equally in the wealth of the nation. Communism, which emerged in the 1840s, was often initially synonymous with socialism, but intellectuals Karl Marx (1818–1883) and Friedrich Engels (1820–1895) offered a new interpretation in their book, *The Communist Manifesto* (1848). The pair's book, the touchstone for communist revolution worldwide, argues that industrialization would bring on the proletarian revolution—or uprising of the working classes. This, in turn, would lead to the abolition of exploitation, private property, and a class society. Communist ideology reemerged with the Russian Revolution in 1917. The term is associated with the form of government practiced by the Soviet Union in the twentieth century, though its government was never fully communist. *See also* Marxism.

compagnia Long-term commercial ventures undertaken by extended families in northern and central Italy in the eleventh and twelfth centuries. Official, legal enterprises, compagnia were established to finance long- and short-distance, land-based trade. Debts and losses were shared equally by all members, which promoted family solidarity but risked bankrupting an entire family in tough times.

concentration camps Internment centers for people imprisoned for their ethnicity or their political beliefs or actions rather than for specific criminal offenses. These were first widely used by the British during the Boer War (1899–1902) to contain Afrikaners within what is now South Africa, but the most infamous versions were created by Nazi Germany as early as 1933. Nazi concentration camps were gradually transformed into extermination centers during World War II (1939–1945), used for the wholesale slaughter of Jews, gypsies, and other "undesirables."

Concert of Europe An agreement by the Great Powers of Europe—Great Britain, Prussia, Russia, Austria, and, after 1818, France—following the Congress of Vienna in 1815 in which they agreed to act together on matters affecting all of them individually. Brokered by the British foreign minister Lord Castlereagh, this arrangement called for regular, informal meetings to maintain stability and special sessions in times of crisis to prevent European war. It helped maintain general peace during the revolutions of 1848. *See also* Congress of Vienna.

Conciliar movement   A reform movement in the late fourteenth and early fifteenth centuries that tried to shift authority in spiritual matters from the papacy to a general council representing the faithful. The movement emerged during the Avignon papacy (1303–1378), when civil strife forced the pope from Rome into this Roman Empire region close to France. After much confusion in which three different councils named three different popes, conciliarism was eventually condemned, and papal supremacy reasserted itself in the century that followed.

Confederation of the Rhine   A federation of German states organized under Napoleon I (r. 1804–1814) in July 1806. Formerly under the rule of the Holy Roman Empire, which was dissolved the same year, the Confederation of the Rhine placed itself under the "protection" of Napoleon and was governed by one of his close allies. It quickly fell apart after Napoleon's defeat outside Leipzig in 1813 as member states abandoned the French and joined the German nationalist "war of liberation."

Congress of Vienna   A meeting among the powers allied against French emperor Napoleon I (r. 1804–1814)—Russia, Prussia, and Austria—that began shortly before his downfall in 1814 and lasted into the following year. Reactionary in many aspects, the congress sought wherever possible to restore Europe to the way it was before the wars of the French Revolution (1789–1799) and Napoleon by returning many states to their traditional monarchs. The congress system, also called the "congress of Europe," helped maintain peace in Europe until the 1850s. *See also* Concert of Europe.

conservatism   A political ideology that emerged after 1815 and sought to restore Europe to the way it was politically and socially before the French Revolution (1789–1799) and the wars of Napoleon. It rejected much of Enlightenment and revolutionary ideology, preferring monarchies over republics, tradition over revolution, and established religion over Enlightenment skepticism. Conservatism was the dominant ideology in several European states throughout the nineteenth century. *See also* Enlightenment.

consorteria   A contractual Italian family arrangement in which all male members shared the profits of the family's inheritance and female members were excluded. First appearing in post-Carolingian Italy (c. tenth century B.C.E.), consorterias arose to prevent dividing up family property into increasingly smaller parcels among heirs. This organization became a model for the development of later Italian businesses and banks.

constitutionalism A system of government in which rulers are required to share power with parliaments made up of elected representatives. Constitutionalism emerged in the seventeenth century and posed a great challenge to absolutism. It was most successful in England, where the Parliament won constitutional concessions from the monarchy as a result of a civil war from 1642–1646 and the Glorious Revolution of 1688. John Locke, whose *Two Treatises of Government* were published in 1690 to justify the Glorious Revolution, used the contemporary notion of a social contract between a government and its people as a foundation of constitutionalism. *See also* absolutism.

consul The title given to the three leaders of the French government installed after the fall of the Directory in 1799. The three consuls theoretically shared power, but Napoleon I as First Consul, later emperor (r. 1804–1814), effectively held uncontested authority and asserted himself as leader in drafting a new constitution, France's fourth since 1789. The word *consul* refers to the system of government in ancient Rome, where two consuls shared executive power. *See also* Directory; First Consul.

consumer revolution An economic shift in the early eighteenth century in which global trade transformed European consumption habits by making widely available new staples previously beyond the reach of ordinary citizens. Trade in the Atlantic and Asian worlds made consumer items such as sugar, tea, chocolate, and coffee increasingly available and affordable to the general public, and economic expansion and population growth further fueled market demand. The result was a dramatic transformation of European society and culture.

consumerism The belief that the purchase of material goods leads to happiness and fulfillment. Consumerism also refers to an economic movement that gained momentum in the post–World War II era (after 1945), suggesting that greater consumption of goods would strengthen the economy.

Continental System Napoleon's order in 1806 that prohibited France, its satellites, dependent states, and allies from purchasing British goods. Britain was the only power standing between Napoleon I (r. 1804–1814) and total dominance of Europe, and the Continental System was meant to isolate Britain and starve its economy. After some early successes in blocking British trade, the system was undermined by smuggling and ultimately proved impossible to enforce.

conversos Spanish term for Jews in the Iberian peninsula who converted to Christianity in the fifteenth century. Conversos were often targeted by the Spanish Inquisition because they were suspected of practicing Judaism in secret while pretending to adhere to Christianity.

Corn Laws Tariffs on grain in Great Britain that benefited landowners by preventing the import of cheap foreign grain. After agitation by the powerful Anti–Corn Law League, which established local branches and published newspapers and the journal *The Economist* (founded in 1843) to garner widespread opposition to the laws, the tariffs were repealed by the British government in 1846.

Council for Mutual Economic Assistance (COMECON) An organization established by the Soviet Union in 1949 to co-ordinate economic development and relations between the Soviet Union and its satellite nations. A fan of U.S. industrial know-how, Communist leader Joseph Stalin urged all socialist economies to match U.S. productivity through this council. In practice, however, it served to bolster the Soviet Union at the expense of the other nations.

Council of Four Hundred The branch of Athenian government created by Solon (c. 630–c. 560 B.C.E.) circa 594 B.C.E. to prepare the legislative assembly's agenda and keep the democracy running efficiently. Confirming the poorest class's right to participate in the assembly, Solon prevented potential corruption and domination by elites, selecting council members by lottery. Around 500 B.C.E., the council was expanded from four hundred to five hundred members.

Council of Trent A series of meetings of the leadership of the Roman Catholic church that took place in the northern Italian town of Trent between 1545 and 1563. Initially called to address and condemn the threat of Protestantism, the council instituted several reforms that shaped the character of Catholicism until the 1960s. It provided for better training and supervision of the clergy, clarified church doctrine, reaffirmed papal authority, and reasserted the supremacy of the clergy over the laity.

Crimean War A conflict from 1853 to 1856 between Russia and the Ottoman Empire over Russia's inroads into territory in Asia and the Middle East and Tsar Nicholas I's (r. 1825–1855) desire to absorb much of Ottoman-controlled lands. Russia was eventually defeated, but not before the casualty rate reached the highest level of any European conflict since the French Revolution (1789–1799) and Napoleonic wars in 1815 to the outbreak of World War I (1914–1918). Significantly, it was the first major conflict to be documented with photographs and reported through the newspapers back to Europe via the telegraph. With the high casualty rate came a movement for nursing reform, prompted by British wartime nurse Florence Nightingale (1820–1910).

crusader states The name given to several tiny states along the eastern coast of the Mediterranean Sea carved out by the participants of the First Crusade. By 1109, these included the County of Edessa, the County of Tripoli, the Principality of Antioch, and the Kingdom of Jerusalem. Because most European rulers were unwilling to commit the resources necessary to defend these states adequately, by 1291 all were permanently back in the hands of the Muslims. *See also* crusades.

crusades Holy wars supported and sometimes proclaimed by the papacy to advance Christianity. Historians cite two main reasons behind the First Crusade: efforts to reform the church from within and the weak state of the papacy generally. The early crusades (1096–1098) sent up to 100,000 European Christians into battle against Muslims in the Holy Land, where they believed Christ had lived and died. Eight major crusades were fought between 1096 and the end of the thirteenth century, but without a European commitment to maintain the crusader states, they fell to the Muslims permanently in 1291. Some groups on crusading journeys robbed and massacred Jews along the way.

Crystal Palace An elaborate glass and iron structure built to house the Great Exhibition of the Works of Industry of All Nations in London in 1851. The edifice, over a third of a mile long, displayed the impact of Britain's industrial growth and technological innovation and generated national pride. It inspired a series of international exhibitions, or world's fairs, over the nineteenth and twentieth centuries. *See also* Great Exhibition.

Cuban missile crisis The cold war confrontation in 1962 between the United States and the Soviet Union over USSR installation of medium-range missiles in Cuba, just off the U.S. coast. The incident nearly brought both nations to the brink of a nuclear disaster. U.S. president John F. Kennedy (1960–1963) responded by calling for a blockade of ships headed for Cuba and threatening a nuclear war if the missiles were not removed. After seven tense days, Kennedy and Soviet Premier Nikita Khrushchev backed down from using nuclear weapons to resolve the situation and instead negotiated an end to the crisis. Kennedy and Khrushchev then dedicated themselves to improving nuclear diplomacy. *See also* cold war.

cult of the offensive A military strategy of constantly attacking the enemy, believed to be the key to winning World War I (1914–1918). Despite the development of new weaponry and war technology in the early twentieth century, this old-fashioned vision of war made many officers unwilling to abandon more traditional—and far less effective—sabers, lances, and bayonets for more modern machine guns and other weapons. Consequently, this strategy boosted casualties and failed to bring victory to either side.

cuneiform A form of writing using wedge-shaped symbols pressed into clay tablets first developed by the Sumerians around 3500 B.C.E. to document their increasingly complex economic transactions. Cuneiform was later used to preserve oral traditions such as storytelling.

curials Members of the social elite in Roman Empire towns who were obligated to serve as unsalaried city council members and spend their own funds to support the community. Under the rule of Diocletian (r. 284–305 C.E.), this support included paying for soldiers, repairing urban structures, and making up for shortfalls in tax collection. As taxes continued to rise, this financial obligation proved financially damaging to local elites.

cynicism From the Greek for "like a dog"; a philosophy that rejected the conventions and comforts of ordinary life, especially wealth and material comfort, regarded self-sufficiency and virtue as the ultimate goals, and believed that anything natural was good and should therefore be done without shame. The most famous early Cynic, Diogenes (c. 323 B.C.E.), slept in a storage jar and wore only borrowed or tattered clothing.

czar *See* tsar.

D

daguerreotype The first successful form of photography, developed in the 1830s by French artist Jacques Daguerre (1789–1851). The daguerreotype transferred a positive image onto a silver plate; its popularity expanded rapidly, filling growing middle-class demand for family portraits at a more reasonable cost than portrait paintings.

Danelaw The region in England settled by the Vikings, who were also known as Danes. The Vikings had previously raided England often; in 876 C.E., however, they settled into the Danelaw, began farming, and forced other English kingdoms to pay a tribute known as the *Danegeld.*

Dark Age A term used by historians to describe a period of social decline, economic depression, and depopulation. Both Greece and the Near East endured widespread violence that sparked Dark Ages; the one in the Near East was relatively short, enduring for less than a century, while the Greek Dark Age lasted from 1000 to 750 B.C.E.

debasement of coinage Using less silver in making coins without changing their corresponding face value. This was practiced by some emperors during the third-century economic crisis in Rome with the hope of creating more cash from the same yield of precious metal. The strategy failed, however, because merchants raised their prices to account for the debased value of coins, producing increased inflation.

Decembrist Revolt of 1825 An uprising over the disputed succession to the Russian throne upon the death of Alexander I (r. 1801–1825). Named for the month in which it occurred, the revolt began when soldiers took sides over which of Alexander's brothers, Constantine or Nicholas, should succeed him. While the majority expected Nicholas to become the new tsar, a rebel group favored Constantine on the throne, believing he would be more sympathetic to constitutional reform. Constantine, however, had already renounced his claim to the throne. The revolt was quickly put down, but the subsequent trial and hard labor imposed on the rebels made them into legendary heroes.

de-Christianization The social and political campaign of extremist republicans in eighteenth-century revolutionary France to limit the influence of religion in daily life. Many churches, both Catholic and Protestant, were closed; clergy were forced to abandon their vocations and marry; and church buildings were auctioned off. Christian holidays and festivals were replaced with patriotic festivals, and extremist groups sought to replace Christianity with secular belief systems, such as the deistic Cult of Reason in 1793. De-Christianization had only limited success, especially in the countryside where rural citizens held fast to traditional religious practices.

Declaration of the Rights of Man and Citizen A decree granting basic rights to French citizens that was written in August 1789 after the French Revolution (1789–1799) as a preamble to France's constitution. Reminiscent of the American Declaration of Independence, this French document established the sovereignty of the nation, meaning that the king derived his authority from the people of the nation rather than from divine right or tradition. It proclaimed that "Men are born and remain free and equal in rights" and granted freedom of religion, freedom of the press, equality in taxation, and the equality of all citizens before the law. Women were theoretically citizens under civil law but did not have the right to full political participation. Slaves were also overlooked in the Declaration.

decolonization The process—both violent and peaceful—by which colonies gained their independence from the imperial powers, primarily after World War II (1939–1945). People in Asia, Africa, and the Middle East, often led by individuals steeped in Western values and experienced in manufacturing and military technology, embraced the cause of independence from their colonizing nations. The relationship between former imperial powers and former colonies has been a significant force in shaping late twentieth- and early twenty-first-century international relations.

decurions Municipal senate members in the Roman Empire responsible for collecting local taxes. Because they were provincial elites and prestigious members of their communities, they were expected to make up the difference themselves if there was a shortfall.

defenestration of Prague An incident in the Bohemian province of the Holy Roman Empire that sparked the Thirty Years' War (1618–1648). In May 1618, two imperial officials were thrown from a window of the royal palace in Prague when they tried to dissolve a meeting of Calvinist leaders as part of a larger effort to curtail Protestant religious freedoms. (The word *defenestration* comes from the French word *fenêtre* meaning "window"). Although the officials suffered only minor injuries, the incident was viewed as an act of rebellion against imperial authority, and Emperor Ferdinand II (Bohemia, Holy Roman emperor; r. 1619–1637) sent troops in response.

degeneration A sense that a species or society is in a state of decline. Toward the end of the nineteenth century, some began to believe that cultural trends such as modern art and social trends such as declining birthrates indicated that Western civilization was in decline. They urged imperial expansion and increased population as the means of reversing this descent. *See also* modernism.

deist A person who believes in God but does not believe that God has an active role in human affairs. Deists believe that a benevolent, all-knowing God designed the universe and set it in motion but no longer intervenes in its functioning. Deism emerged in the West during the eighteenth-century Enlightenment, as scientists and philosophers discovered natural explanations for how the universe operated that did not rely on divine intervention. *See also* atheist; Enlightenment.

Delian League The naval alliance of Greek city-states headed by Athens after the Persian Wars (499–479 B.C.E.) and the basis of the Athenian Empire. Following the Greek defeat of the Persians in 479 B.C.E., many city-states feared further hostility and invasion. Named for the island of Delos where its treasury was kept, the Delian League came to be dominated by Athenians, who used its revenue to glorify their city.

demes Greek for "people"; a new Athenian political system established by Cleisthenes c. 500 B.C.E. in which citizens were organized into constituencies by country villages and urban neighborhoods. Demes chose council members annually by lottery in proportion to the size of their populations, ensuring greater citizen participation in government.

demography The study of the size, growth, density, distribution, and vital statistics of a human population. Demography is useful for conceptualizing historical change and often includes a focus on shifting patterns of life expectancy, births, deaths, marriages, and residence or settlement patterns. It can also reflect lifestyle changes and trends, including distribution of wealth and labor.

département An administrative unit developed in revolutionary France, intended to minimize regional distinctions and provide a more efficient and egalitarian government. Départements were to be equal in size and provide all inhabitants with easy access to government services. All officials were elected, and no offices could be bought or sold. The départements remain the basic units of the French state today.

détente From the French for "loosening or relaxing"; an easing of tensions between rivals. Most commonly used to refer to the lessening of cold war tensions between the United States and the Soviet Union in the late 1960s and the 1970s. Global instability encouraged both superpowers to limit the nuclear arms race, which formed the basis for the détente.

diaspora From the Greek for "scatter, disperse, or spread about"; dispersion of people from their homelands. Although other cultures have experienced diasporas, the term most often refers to the expulsion of the Jews from their homeland in ancient Israel. Many Jews settled among the Assyrians (722 B.C.E.) and neo-Babylonians (586 B.C.E.), preserving their cultural and religious traditions in exile. Other Jewish Diasporas occurred throughout history, notably after Jews rebelled against Rome in the first and second centuries C.E. The Persian king Cyrus (c. 593 B.C.E.) allowed the Jews to return from exile to their homeland after 593 B.C.E., where they were allowed to rebuild their temple and practice their religion. But they remained subject to various Near Eastern powers. The slave trade (1450–1870) created an African diaspora throughout Europe and its colonies.

dictator In ancient Rome, a political official who was granted total authority for a limited time as a temporary stopgap to thwart political crisis. However, Roman generals such as Sulla (c. 138–78 B.C.E.) were able to obtain the rank without term limits and abuse its power for personal gain. In modern times, dictators similarly came to, and in some cases seized, power during crises, but once there often discarded or replaced existing laws and political structures. Examples include Adolf Hitler (1889–1945), who rose to power in Germany in 1934, and Benito Mussolini (1883–1945), who similarly took control in Italy in 1922.

Diplomatic Revolution A shift in European alliances in 1756 that reshaped relations among the great powers at the start of the Seven Years' War (1756–1763). It began when Great Britain and Prussia, Britain's former adversary during the War of Austrian Succession (1740–1748), signed a defensive alliance, prompting Austria to overlook two centuries of hostility and ally with France. Russia and Sweden, enemies three decades earlier in the Great Northern War of 1721, also joined the alliance.

Directory The political body that governed France between the fall of Maximilien Robespierre (1758–1794) in 1794 and the rise of Napoleon I (r. 1804–1814) in 1799. Designed to keep a single person from wielding too much power, the Directory was an executive body comprised of five directors instituted by the new constitution. It faced many challenges from remaining Jacobins and royalists. Napoleon's supporters toppled it with relative ease and replaced it with a three-man consulate in which Napoleon was the First Consul. *See also* consul; Jacobin Club.

DNA Abbreviation for deoxyribonucleic acid, the genetic material that forms the basis of each cell. The discovery of DNA structure in 1952 by James Watson, an American, and Francis Crick, an Englishman, revolutionized genetics, molecular biology, and other scientific and medical fields.

domesticity The set of beliefs, prevailing in the early to mid-nineteenth century, that purported that women should live their lives within the domestic sphere and devote themselves to their families and the home. In reality, the notion of a separate domestic sphere for women rendered them economically dependent on men and prevented them from pursuing higher education, gaining paid employment in the professions, or participating in politics by holding office or voting—all activities deemed appropriate only for men.

Dominate The name given by historians to Roman imperial rule from Diocletian (r. 284–305 C.E.) onward because of its leaders' claims to supreme power. To solidify his power, Diocletian took the title of *lord* (in Latin, *dominus*), thus abandoning the long-standing republican title of *princeps* (meaning "first man"). From Diocletian on, the office of emperor assumed an aggressively autocratic nature, eliminating any sharing of authority with the Senate and recognizing no social equals.

Dual Alliance A defensive alliance forged by German chancellor Otto von Bismarck between Germany and Austria-Hungary in 1879 as part of his system of alliances to prevent or limit war. When Italy joined in 1882 as a third partner, it was renamed the Triple Alliance.

dual monarchy A shared power arrangement between the Habsburg Empire and Hungary that was developed after the Prussian defeat of the Austrian Empire in 1867. Essentially, the notion of a dual monarchy was a compromise between Hungary's desire for independence and Emperor Francis Joseph I's goal of creating a strong centralized empire. Francis Joseph (r. 1848–1916) agreed to allow home rule in Hungary—essentially permitting a separate ruler there—because he hoped it would stabilize the empire. Instead, it served as a roadblock to unity since other national groups such as the Czechs and Slovaks subsequently voiced similar demands for self-rule.

dualism   The belief that the spiritual and physical beings are separate. Established by the Greek philosopher Plato (c. 429–348 B.C.E.), dualism stresses that humans possess immortal souls distinct from their bodies and that the soul possesses preexisting knowledge put there by a deity.

duchy   A state ruled by dukes. During the Renaissance, Italian states were either governed as republics, which preserved traditional institutions of medieval communes ruled by a civic elite, or principalities ruled by a dynasty. Florence in what is now the Italian Republic, for example, became a duchy in 1530 under the Medici family.

Duma   The Russian parliament set up in the aftermath of the outbreak of the Revolution of 1905. Although few Russians could actually vote for representatives, the Duma's existence, coupled with the right of public political debate, promised all classes a liberalized government and an opportunity to present their grievances.

dynatoi   A new hereditary elite, largely comprised of military families, that developed in the Byzantine Empire during the tenth and eleventh centuries. These families grew increasingly powerful from the new lands and other property taken in the empire's conquests.

E

early modern The term historians use to describe the period between the European Middle Ages and the Industrial Revolution. Historians generally place the early modern period between 1500 and 1800. The early modern period saw the emergence of secularization and scientific thinking, which represented a turn away from the supernatural and spiritually driven worldview of the Middle Ages.

economic miracle Generally, Europe's rapid recovery from the devastation of World War II (1939–1945); in particular, Germany's striking prosperity despite military defeat.

Edict of Milan The proclamation of religious tolerance throughout the Roman Empire issued in 313 by the emperors Constantine (r. 306–337 C.E.), a recent convert to Christianity, and Licinius (r. 308–324 C.E.), a follower of traditional Roman religion. The edict, which abolished restrictions on Christianity, was prompted by Constantine's conversion. Although he secretly hoped to promote Christianity, he astutely sought religious tolerance instead, to avoid angering traditional believers who outnumbered Christians.

Edict of Nantes A treaty signed in 1598 by King Henry IV (r. 1589–1610) of France ending decades of religious conflict by granting French Protestants, or Huguenots, limited religious freedoms and toleration. This shift in royal policy represented a significant trend in which the interests of the state prevailed over all other concerns, including religious ideals. The edict remained in effect until Louis XIV (r. 1643–1715) revoked it in 1685. *See also* Huguenots.

Edict on Maximum Prices Diocletian's harsh system of wage and price controls. In 301 the Roman emperor Diocletian (r. 284–305 C.E.) sought to combat the hyperinflation caused by previous civil wars by forbidding the hoarding of goods and coins and controlling the prices of over one thousand goods and services. The edict proved unsuccessful, however, because merchants were unwilling to cooperate and government officials were unable to enforce it. *See also* Dominate.

educational reform Beginning in the nineteenth century, European nations, initially Germany and Britain, began to take control of primary and secondary education, removing control from religious bodies. Part of nation building, the goal was to make the general population more fit for citizenship and able to contribute to economic expansion. To increase literacy, governments passed laws mandating schooling for children. There was also a shift in the kind of knowledge deemed necessary as state entities assumed responsibility for education. Instead of teaching the Bible, as was the case when religious authorities oversaw education, secular leaders called for studies that stressed what workers needed to know to become good citizens: the language, literature, history of their nation. These actions led to significant rises in literacy by the end of the nineteenth century.

EEC *See* European Economic Community.

elector One of seven officials charged with choosing a German king in the Holy Roman Empire. According to the terms agreed to in the Golden Bull of 1356, an edict stamped with the golden seal of the ruler, these officials had to be ecclesiastical and secular princes and included the king of Bohemia; the archbishops of Mainz, Trier, and Cologne; the duke of Saxony-Wittenberg; the margrave of Brandenburg; and the count palatine of the Rhine. The electors had great influence over the emperor because they determined whether his son would succeed him.

emigration The process by which people leave their homeland and seek permanent residence in another country. Large numbers of people from Europe and Asia emigrated beginning in the mid-nineteenth century. The United States was the most popular destination for many people hoping to find better opportunities abroad than existed for them at home.

empire A political unit in which one or more formerly independent territories or people are governed by a single sovereign power. The world's first empire was created by the conquests of the Akkadian king Sargon (c. 2350 B.C.E.), who ruled over territory stretching from Sumer to the Mediterranean Sea. An unintended consequence of many empires, including Sargon's, was the cultural interaction between the various peoples of the new state, who adopted and adapted some of each other's beliefs, traditions, and literature.

empiricism A philosophical doctrine that emphasizes the role of observation, experimentation, and deductive reasoning in the acquisition of knowledge. Although this approach to knowledge dates back to philosophers such as Aristotle (384–322 B.C.E.), in its modern sense, it is associated with the scientific method developed by seventeenth-century intellectual Francis Bacon

(1561–1626) of England and René Descartes (1596–1650) of France. It represented a significant turn away from traditional thinking with its reliance on classical philosophy and the Scriptures. *See also* idealism.

Ems telegram   An altered telegram sent from Prussia by Otto von Bismarck on July 13, 1870, in the name of Prussian king William I (r. 1861–1888), designed to incense the French. William I had been approached by the French ambassador at the resort town of Ems regarding France's unhappiness with Spain's consideration of a minor Prussian prince to fill a vacancy on the Spanish throne. The French worried about having Prussian rulers on two of its borders (the other being Germany). With the hope of sparking nationalist sentiment in both countries, Bismarck changed the tone of King William's response to French concerns to make it appear an insult to France. In response, the French demanded war, and the Franco-Prussian War began on July 19, 1870. *See also* Franco-Prussian War.

Enabling Act   German legislation passed in 1933 suspending constitutional government for four years to tackle the economic crisis in Germany. It allowed Nazi laws to take effect without parliamentary approval and ultimately made Adolf Hitler's rise to dictator legally possible.

enclosure movement   A trend during the agricultural revolution in eighteenth-century England in which wealthy landowners consolidated their holdings by pressuring small farmers to sell their land or give up grazing rights to common lands. As a result, the English peasant class effectively disappeared, replaced by a more hierarchical rural society with wealthy landlords at the top, tenant farmers in the middle, and poor laborers at the bottom.

enlightened despots   European rulers who sought to apply some of the reforms of the eighteenth-century Enlightenment to their governments without giving up their own absolutist authority. Enlightened despotism is characterized by legal, administrative, and educational improvements when it suited the state and as a means to enhance its power. Examples of enlightened despots include Frederick the Great of Prussia (r. 1740–1786), Catherine the Great of Russia (r. 1762–1796), and Joseph II of Austria (r. 1780–1790).

Enlightenment   The eighteenth-century intellectual movement whose proponents believed that political, social, and economic problems could be solved through the application of reason and critical thinking. Based on the popularization of scientific discoveries and increased literacy, the Enlightenment often challenged religious and secular authorities by questioning traditional knowledge and the status quo. However, many European monarchs patronized Enlightenment thinkers and tried to apply Enlightenment principles to state reforms. The Enlightenment was most prominent in France, although it spread throughout Europe and North America. *See also* enlightened despots.

Entente Cordiale   An alliance between Britain and France that began with a secret agreement in 1904 to honor each other's colonial holdings, in particular Britain's claims in Egypt and France's claims in Morocco.

Epic of Gilgamesh   A long poem written circa 2500 B.C.E. about the adventures of the hero Gilgamesh. Written in cuneiform, it tells the story of King Gilgamesh and his search for immortality. A later version includes a description of a great flood that covered the earth, foreshadowing the biblical account of Noah's ark. The version that exists today is a combination of many variations of the original tale. *See also* cuneiform.

Epicureanism   The Greek philosophy initiated by Epicurus of Athens (341–271 B.C.E.) to help people achieve pleasure in their lives, free of worry about death. Epicurus defined pleasure as the "absence of disturbance," meaning that people should lead sober lives spent with friends and separated from daily distractions of turbulence, passions, and ordinary desires. He challenged traditional notions of Greek citizenship by allowing women and slaves to study in his group and embracing women's participation in public and religious cults.

epigrams   Short poems covering a variety of themes, especially love, and a favorite genre of women poets from diverse regions of Greece during the Hellenist Age (323–30 B.C.E.). The poet Nossi of Locri, for example, dedicated her best-known verse to the power of Eros, the Greek god of love.

equites   An early Roman republic social class of landowners and businessmen wealthy enough to provide horses for the cavalry and whose careers in commerce set them at odds with senators in the government. They emerged as a powerful political force against the Senate under the tribune, or leader, Gaius Gracchus (123 B.C.E.), when equites were appointed to serve on juries and could convict criminal senators.

Estates General   A body of deputies representing the three estates, or orders, of France: the clergy (First Estate), the nobility

(Second Estate), and everyone else (Third Estate). The Estates General originated in the fourteenth century as an advisory body but fell out of use after 1614 when the French monarchy adopted a more absolutist style of rule. A fiscal crisis forced Louis XVI (1774–1792) to summon the estates in 1789, and disputes about procedures of voting in this body paved the way for the French Revolution (1789–1799).

ethnic cleansing The mass murder—genocide—of people of different ethnicities during the wars that developed when states declared themselves independent from Yugoslavia in the 1990s. Today the term refers to any attempts at genocide.

EU *See* European Union.

eugenics The pseudoscience founded by Sir Francis Galton in the late nineteenth century that sought to improve the quality of the human race. Eugenics was based on a discriminatory set of beliefs that some people were better fit to breed the next generation of human beings. The so-called fittest included the wealthy and educated; those considered unfit were usually lower class, mentally ill, physically disabled, or nonwhite. Eugenics became popular in Nazi Germany in the 1930s, where some of its tenets, especially those related to racial superiority, were put into practice. Other governments around the world similarly enacted laws based on eugenics, including those banning interracial marriage and forcing sterilization of those deemed mentally and physically disabled. *See also* Social Darwinism.

euro The common currency accepted by twelve of the fifteen members of the European Union. It went into effect gradually, becoming the currency of business transfers in 1999 and entering public circulation across most of Europe in 2002.

European Economic Community (EEC, or Common Market) A consortium of six European countries—Belgium, France, Italy, Luxembourg, the Netherlands, and West Germany (now Germany)—established to promote free trade and economic cooperation among its members. The EEC brought under one umbrella more than 200 million consumers at its founding in 1957 and subsequently added several hundred million more. Such growth and cooperation offered great economic benefits to members and expanded the consortium's size and sphere of activity.

European Union (EU) A unified association of European countries formed in 1994 to end national distinctions in spheres of business activity, border controls, and transportation.

It evolved from the European Economic Community (EEC, or Common Market) and the European Community that was originally established two years earlier by the Maastricht Treaty. EU members have political ties through the European parliament as well as long-standing common economic, legal, and business mechanisms. In 1999, the EU united its members with a common currency, the euro. As of 2006, it consisted of twenty-five member countries. *See also* euro; Maastricht Treaty.

Evangelicals Supporters of Martin Luther's quest for religious reform within the Catholic church in the 1520s. The word *Evangelical* refers to the Gospels and emphasizes Luther's strict adherence to the Bible as a source of religious authority and doctrine. After 1529, Luther and his followers were known as Protestants, in reference to a protest lodged against imperial authorities who had declared Luther's reform movement criminal.

evolution The scientific theory that life took shape over millions of years and that human life was not the result of divine creation but rather of a slow and changing biological process. At its core, the theory embraces the concept of natural selection and argues that human life emerged from lower forms through a primal struggle for survival in which some species were able to adapt and others died off. Although ideas of evolutionary change predate British scientist Charles Darwin (1809–1882), the publication of his *On the Origin of Species* in 1859 placed the issue at the forefront of political and scientific debate.

existentialism A literary and philosophical movement popular after World War II (1939–1945) that explores the meaning (or lack of meaning) of human existence in a world where evil seems to triumph and God seems absent. Existentialists address the question of "being," arguing that God does not endow spiritual goodness or determine the nature of a person's existence, but rather that the individual, through action and choice, creates his or her authentic self. Frenchmen Jean-Paul Sartre (1905–1980) and Albert Camus (1913–1960) were among its most notable adherents.

exposure An accepted ancient Greek and Roman practice of abandoning infants when parents could not or would not raise them. This act was not considered infanticide because parents expected someone else to find and raise the abandoned children. Infant girls were the more likely victims of exposure; estimates claim up to 10 percent of nonwealthy Greek girls were exposed.

F

Fall of Rome Historical label for the aftermath of the deposition of the Roman emperor Romulus Augustulus (r. 475–476 C.E.). Following a dispute over pay in 476, non-Roman soldiers removed Romulus Augustulus from the throne and murdered his father. The leader of the rebels, Odoacer, chose not to appoint a new emperor in his place, leading to the creation of the term *Fall of Rome*. Scholars today consider it more accurate to label this period a *transformation* rather than a *fall*.

family allowance Government funds provided to families to help cover the cost of raising children. It was used in totalitarian and democratic countries alike to boost the birthrate in the 1930s.

fascism A doctrine advocated and named by Italian leader Benito Mussolini (1883–1945) in 1922 that glorified the state over individual or civil rights. Beginning in the 1920s, fascism was politically grounded in an instinctual male violence and opposed to the antinationalist socialist movement and parliamentary rule.

feminism A social and political movement seeking equality for women and an end to all forms of gender discrimination. Though the term was first used in the early twentieth century, *feminism* has come to signify the tenets of the worldwide women's movement that emerged in the 1960s and 1970s. Feminism argues for, among other things, complete gender equity in the workplace, women's right to control their bodies via access to birth control and safe and legal abortions, and a ban on the use of physiological differences to block women from opportunities in employment, education, and sports. *See also* women's movement.

Fertile Crescent The geographic region in southwestern Asia that stretches in an arc from modern Israel across Syria to southern Iraq along the Tigris and Euphrates rivers. The region's name indicates its ideal combination of soil, water, and temperature, which facilitated the growth of crops for food and, subsequently, the development of agriculture and the domestication of animals (10,000–8000 B.C.E.). The Fertile Crescent is also home to several early civilizations and the first large cities, among them Sumer, Babylonia, and Assyria.

feudalism A word used by some historians to explain the social, economic, and political hierarchy in western Europe during the Middle Ages. Historians disagree on its precise usage; some use it to describe an economy of peasants dominated by nobility, while others define it as a relationship of obligation between lord and vassal.

First Consul The most important of the three consuls, or leaders, established by the French Constitution of 1799, which named Napoleon Bonaparte as First Consul. The word *consul* refers to the system of government in the Roman republic, where two consuls shared executive power. The three consuls theoretically shared power, but as First Consul, Napoleon held uncontested authority. *See also* consul.

First Triumvirate An arrangement made in 60 B.C.E. between the three most powerful Roman political figures—Pompey, Crassus, and Caesar—to gain concessions for themselves. Pompey received land for his soldiers and passed laws that confirmed his affairs in the east; Crassus gained financial relief for the Roman tax collectors in Asia Minor who supported him; and Caesar secured the counsulship in 59 B.C.E. and a command in Gaul.

Five Good Emperors The term used to describe the rule of five of the most successful emperors in Roman history. The reign of Nerva (96–98 C.E.), Trajan (98–117 C.E.), Hadrian (117–138 C.E.), Antoninus Pius (138–161 C.E.), and Marcus Aurelius (161–180 C.E.) is often regarded by historians as a "golden age" of Roman history, marked by peaceful transfers of imperial power, prosperity, and strong economic and population growth.

five pillars Five key practices held as central tenets of the Islamic faith instituted by Muhammad (c. 570–632 C.E.). They are zakat, a tax used for alms; hajj, a pilgrimage to Mecca that each Muslim must make once in his or her lifetime; salat, formal worship several times per day; shahadah, the profession of faith; and the fast of Ramadan, the ninth month of the Islamic calendar.

five-year plans Centralized programs for long-range economic development first used by Joseph Stalin (1879–1953) in the Soviet Union in 1929 and copied by Adolf Hitler (1889–1945) in Germany; these plans outlined a program to boost the economy by setting production goals for agriculture and individual industries, among them coal, iron ore, and steel.

flagellants Roving bands of Christians who whipped themselves in public as a form of penance during the Black Death in the mid-fourteenth century. The Black Death, a devastatingly lethal plague, was perceived as a divine punishment, and the flagellants believed that by whipping themselves they would appease God's wrath. Secular and religious people alike looked on them with suspicion because they did not originate within the church hierarchy and attracted people from the margins of society. They often incited popular violence, particularly against Jews, and were declared heretical in 1350.

Fourteen Points A proposal by U.S. president Woodrow Wilson (1913–1921) for peace during World War I (1914–1918). The Fourteen Points called for peace based on settlement rather than on victory or a definitive conquest and thus helped bring about the surrender of the Central Powers. Wilson called for open diplomacy, arms reduction, flexibility in resolving colonial issues, and the self-determination of peoples.

Fourth Lateran Council The church council, appointed by Pope Innocent III (r. 1198–1216) in 1215 that attempted to regulate all aspects of Christian life. With a goal of reforming both the clergy and the laity, canons of the council codified traditions of marriage, strengthened the importance of the Eucharist and the sacraments, called for all Jews to advertise their religion with some outward sign (usually a badge, but sometimes a particular style or color of hat or clothing), and condemned heresy.

Franco-Prussian War A war between France and Prussia (1870–1871) in which France was quickly beaten by the newly modernized Prussian army. The war demonstrated the importance of new technologies, such as the train and the telegraph, which the Prussians used to their advantage. The quick defeat signaled a shift in power relations in Europe and was a key moment in the unification of Germany. It was triggered by French concerns about Prussia's growing power at its borders, along with an insulting telegram allegedly sent to France by Prussian king William I (r. 1861–1888). *See also* Ems telegram.

Free Corps Armed citizen militias in the Dutch Patriot Revolt of 1787. The Dutch Patriots sought to limit the powers of the Prince of Orange, who favored ties with Great Britain, and establish a more democratic and independent form of government. The Patriot revolt was put down with the support of Prussian armies.

Freemasons Members of Masonic lodges, social clubs organized around the elaborate secret rituals of stonemasons' guilds. Freemasonry provided a place outside the traditional channels of socializing where nobles and middle-class professionals and even some artisans mingled and shared their common interest in the Enlightenment and reform. The movement began in Great Britain in the early eighteenth century and spread eastward across Europe. Although not explicitly political, Freemasonry encouraged equality among its members. Lodges drew up constitutions and voted in elections, thus promoting a direct experience of constitutional government.

friars Latin for "brothers"; members of the mendicant orders, those who relied on others for their living through alms (donations) or, more typically, begging. The term was originally used for the first mendicant order, the Brothers of St. Francis, or Franciscans, founded by St. Francis of Assisi in the twelfth century, but came to refer to all mendicants.

frieze A continuous band of figures sculpted in relief and found in Greek temples, usually decorating the interior wall of the porch. The Parthenon in Athens (constructed c. 440–430 B.C.E.) has a famous frieze depicting men, women, and children in a procession before the gods.

Fronde A series of revolts in France from 1648 to 1653 that challenged the authority of young King Louis XIV (r. 1643–1715) and his minister Mazarin. Royal power had expanded greatly during the seventeenth century under Mazarin and his mentor Richelieu, fostering resentment among the nobility and the parlements who lost power. The Fronde began when Mazarin attempted to impose a new tax on members of the parlements, who refused to pay. When Mazarin arrested the ringleaders of the resistance, Parisians rebelled, forcing the monarchy to flee the city. The Fronde left a lasting impression on Louis XIV, who designed his policies to prevent future rebellions. *See also* parlements.

G

galley A long, narrow ship propelled primarily by oars that was the main form of sea transportation in the Mediterranean world from ancient times through the seventeenth century. Because galley ships were not well suited for the open ocean, they limited European expansion into the Atlantic until new navigational and shipbuilding technologies were developed in the fourteenth and fifteenth centuries. They required vast crews of rowers, who were often prisoners of war, convicts, or slaves.

Gallicanism From *Gaul*, the ancient Roman name for France; a special arrangement for the Catholic church in France by which the monarchy effectively controlled ecclesiastical revenue and the appointment of bishops in his kingdom. Based on a long medieval tradition, it was formalized by King Charles VII (r. 1422–1461) with the Pragmatic Sanction of Bourges in 1438 and reaffirmed with the Concordat of Bologna in 1516. Although the papacy was recognized as the ultimate authority within the church, Gallicanism gave the French government a greater say in church policy and administration.

Gallo-Romans The Romanized people who remained in Gaul after the end of the western Roman Empire (which fell to the Visigoths c. 418 and largely disappeared by the 530s). The Gallo-Roman elite increasingly merged with the elite of the newer Frankish people. By the sixth century, the two cultures had become strikingly similar, sharing language, settlement patterns, and religious sensibilities. *See also* Romanization.

geniza A storeroom or depository in a Jewish synagogue that houses important documents. Jewish tradition does not allow any document that might contain the name of God to be destroyed; a geniza serves as a cache for these documents until they can receive a ritual cemetery burial. The Cairo geniza, built in 882 and rediscovered in 1890, has provided historians with vital documents about everyday life in the Mediterranean world.

genocide The deliberate and systematic eradication of a group of people because of their race, religion, or nationality, often by a government. The term has been used to refer to the Ottoman Empire's attempts to destroy all Armenians in 1915, Nazi efforts to exterminate the Jews during World War II (1939–1945), the slaughter of Tutsis in Rwanda in 1994, and the killing of Muslims in Yugoslavia in 1995.

Germanic peoples Older scholarly term used to describe the non-Roman peoples who flooded into the late Roman Empire after the fourth century C.E. The term misrepresents the variety of languages and customs among these multiethnic groups, however; the so-called Germanic peoples were a diverse population with no strongly established ethnic identity, and many had had previous contact with the Roman world. Following their arrival in the Roman Empire, many developed separate ethnic identities and formed new societies for themselves and the Romans in their territory.

Girondins (or Girondists) A political party that emerged in revolutionary France after the fall of the monarchy in 1792 when the Jacobins split into two factions. Named for the region in southwestern France where many of their leaders were from, the Girondins were members of the professional class (lawyers and merchants) who wanted a constitutional government, opposed the growing influence of Parisian militants, and championed the smaller provinces beyond the city of Paris. They were the main opposition to the leftist Mountain, which embraced radical counterrevolutionaries. The two groups clashed over workers' demands and especially over the fate of Louis XVI (r. 1774–1792). The Girondins agreed that the king was guilty of treason but were reluctant to execute him, arguing for exile or a referendum on his fate. The Girondins were the first to be targeted at the beginning of the Terror. *See also* Jacobin Club; Mountain; Terror.

gladiators Men who fought in the Roman arena as a form of entertainment. Originally part of extravagant funeral shows, gladiators became popular entertainment for large Roman audiences under the rule of Augustus (r. 27 B.C.E.–14 C.E.). War captives, criminals, slaves, and free volunteers, gladiators were often wounded in their theatrical combat but rarely killed. Victory brought riches and celebrity, but not social respectability.

glasnost Russian for "openness" or "publicity"; a policy instituted in the 1980s by Soviet premier Mikhail Gorbachev calling for greater openness in speech and in thinking, which translated to the reduction of censorship in publishing, radio, television, and other media.

globalization The increasingly interconnected nature of the world in terms of politics, economics, and culture and the decreasing importance of traditional national boundaries. Though it began as early as the sixteenth century, it achieved its greatest impact in the late twentieth and early twenty-first centuries.

Glorious Revolution The revolution in England in 1688 in which the Parliament deposed King James II (r. 1685–1688) and replaced him with his daughter Mary and her husband William, prince of Orange (r. 1689–1702). It was dubbed "Glorious" because it was accomplished with little bloodshed. James II's absolutist rule and pro-Catholic policies had generated resistance in Parliament. The solidly Protestant William and Mary guaranteed a more constitutional form of monarchy in which Parliament had a greater share of state power.

Golden Horde The Mongol Empire in Russia (c. 1241–1480). The Mongols, who captured the city of Kiev in 1240, dominated all of Russia's principalities for about two hundred years. Russian princes could continue to rule as long as they paid homage and tribute to the Mongol khan, or leader. The Russian church was tolerated and exempted from taxes. The term *Golden Horde* probably comes from a combination of the yellowish color of the leader's tent and the Turkish word for "camp."

Gothic A style of architecture characterized by pointed arches, ribbed vaults, and large stained-glass windows that began around 1135. It dates back to the rebuilding of the church of St. Denis by the abbot Suger, who hoped to create a style emphasizing the purity of heaven. Consequently, Gothic architecture is marked by an emphasis on space and light: Exteriors are often dark and forbidding, but the interiors represent lightness, harmony, and order. By the thirteenth century, Gothic architecture had spread from France to other European countries. In the early to mid-nineteenth century, a revival of Gothic art, architecture, and literature looked to the Middle Ages for inspiration. In significant part, due to romanticism, attempts to bring back this style took hold primarily in Britain and the United States. *See also* romanticism.

Great Exhibition The first international exhibition of manufactured goods and the imaginative technologies that produced them, demonstrating the impact of the Industrial Revolution. Held in London in 1851, it was the progenitor of the international exhibitions and world's fairs that took place in the nineteenth and twentieth centuries in the West. Also known as the Crystal Palace Exhibition for the purpose-built structure it was housed in, it was immensely influential economically and culturally. *See also* Crystal Palace.

Great Fear The term used by historians to describe the rural panic during the beginning of the French Revolution (1789–1799). As the National Assembly devised a constitution, people in the countryside, already facing severe food shortages, struggled with rumors about an aristocratic plot to pay beggars and vagrants to burn crops or barns. These rumors sometimes inspired violent attacks on aristocrats or on property holders' records of peasants' dues.

Great Persecution The violent program issued by Diocletian (r. 284–305 C.E.) in 303 to force Christians to convert to traditional Roman religion or risk confiscation of their property, removal from public office, and even death. This persecution was ultimately unsuccessful; violence against Christians often aroused the sympathy of pagans and undermined social stability without eliminating Christianity.

Great Schism A term referring to one of two different ruptures in the history of the Christian church. The first rupture occurred in 1054 between the Roman Catholic church and the Greek Orthodox church; the second took place from 1378 to 1417, when the Catholic church had two claimants to the papacy: one in Rome, Italy, and the other in Avignon, France.

Greek fire A potent military weapon of the Byzantine navy used in the mid-eighth century, comprised of a combustible oil that floated on water and burst into flames when it hit its target. The weapon was responsible for many Byzantine naval victories and enabled the endurance of the Byzantine Empire.

Gregorian chant The music of the Benedictine monastery, consisting of melodies sung in unison without instrumental accompaniment. Also known as plainchant, these melodies probably originated in Rome and were spread throughout Europe by order of Charlemagne (r. 768–814 C.E.), who wanted to standardize liturgical practices in his kingdom. The chant first appeared in written documents of the ninth century; by the twelfth century, a large repertoire of melodies had been recorded.

Gregorian reform The church reform movement associated with Pope Gregory VII (r. 1073–1085). A passionate advocate of papal primacy, Gregory sought reforms that would save the papacy from the vices and evils of worldly rulers and included an end to lay investiture, an emphasis on the sacraments, and clerical celibacy.

Guernica A town in Spain that in 1937 was bombed by German planes during the Spanish Civil War (1936–1939). Considering it an opportunity to test new weapons and practice terror bombing of civilians, German leader Adolf Hitler (1889–

1945) and Italian leader Benito Mussolini (1883–1945) sent military forces in support of Spain's general Francisco Franco (1892–1975). This represented the first significant use of airplanes as bombers and thus anticipated the new military technologies that later became a significant factor in World War II (1939–1945). Pablo Picasso (1881–1973) commemorated the destruction in his mural of the same name.

guilds Associations of craftsmen, merchants, or professionals that often began as religious organizations. By the second half of the twelfth century, however, they became professional associations defined by rules that regulated, protected, and policed their membership. A guild member began his career as an apprentice placed into the tutelage of a master craftsman for a number of years. The apprentice next became a journeyman who worked for a master for a wage. The final rank was master, or craftsman, at which point he owned his own shop and dominated the offices and policies of the guild.

Gulag Russian prison camps. The term was derived from an acronym for the administrative arm of the government that ran the camps. Housing millions of prisoners under lethal conditions, Gulags were created in Soviet Russia in places like Siberia to contain those seen as dissidents or threats to the state. They were first used by V. I. Lenin (1870–1924) in the early twentieth century and, to a much greater extent, by Joseph Stalin (1879–1953) beginning in the 1930s. The extremely harsh conditions included hard labor and lack of adequate food and housing, resulting in the death of up to one million people annually.

H

Hanseatic League From the German word *hansa* for "merchant guild" or "trading association"; a trade alliance that formed in the thirteenth century between major cities and small towns along the Baltic and North seas. The Hanseatic League was centered in Lübeck, Germany, and had almost total control over trade in the Baltic and North seas. It reached the height of its power in the fifteenth century but went into decline in the sixteenth and seventeenth centuries, as it was eclipsed in the region by the English, Dutch, and Swedes.

Hasidim Hebrew for "most pious"; members of a Jewish religious revivalist movement started by Ba'al Shem Tov in the 1740s and 1750s and prominent in Poland-Lithuania. The Hasidim pray in a highly emotional and loud fashion and wear rustic clothing to emphasize their piety. These practices represent a turn away from the formality of traditional synagogues.

Haussmannization The process of urban renewal involving massive public works and the widening of public spaces followed by many governments after the middle of the nineteenth century. It was named after its prime practitioner, the Frenchman Georges-Eugène Haussmann (1809–1891).

heliocentrism The theory that the earth and planets revolve around the sun, proposed by Polish clergyman Nicolaus Copernicus (1473–1543) and accepted in the West in the sixteenth century. Although this idea was first put forth by ancient Greek philosophers, most people continued to believe that the sun and planets revolved around the earth. This theory was originally condemned by the Roman Catholic church for contradicting the notion that the earth was the center of God's creation, a key component of biblical accounts of the Creation.

Hellenistic An adjective meaning "Greek-like" that is today used as a chronological term for the period following Alexander the Great's (r. 336–323 B.C.E.) conquests in the Near East (c. 323–30 B.C.E.). This period was marked by the spread of Greek science, art, philosophy, religion, and culture throughout much of the known world.

Helots Greeks who were captured and enslaved by neighboring Spartans. Most came from Messenia, which Sparta vanquished c. 700 B.C.E. Although they outnumbered free Spartans,

Helots' slave status was maintained through beatings, public humiliation, and legally sanctioned violence. Possessing few rights, Helots labored on farms and in households so that Spartans could focus on military training.

heresy A set of religious beliefs that differ from officially sanctioned dogma. Heresy was perceived as a threat not only to church authority but also to society in general since it was believed that it could provoke God's anger. The idea of heresy existed from the early days of Christianity and was usually dealt with through councils of church leaders who met to determine which beliefs were orthodox. As the papacy grew in power during the high Middle Ages, new methods were devised to detect, prevent, and punish heresy, among them, the Inquisition. *See also* Inquisition; orthodoxy.

hetaira Greek for "companion"; an attractive, witty woman who entertained and performed at symposia (parties at which men drank and discussed intellectual matters). Hetairas were not held to the traditional Greek restrictions for women, were often able to choose their own sexual partners, and enjoyed a freedom of speech that "proper" women did not. Aspasia, the lover and eventual wife of Pericles (c. 495–429 B.C.E.), was the most famous hetaira in Athens.

hierarchy A social organization that ranks certain members as more important, and therefore more dominant, than others. Hierarchies are typically based on wealth, social standing or class, or race. The earliest societies known to use this form of differentiation date back to the Paleolithic era (10,000 B.C.E.).

hieroglyph An Egyptian form of writing that employed pictures or symbols as its characters. One of several scripts used by the Egyptian peoples, hieroglyph was developed during the Old Kingdom period (c. 3050–2190 B.C.E.) and used for official texts. Simplified scripts were later developed for everyday use.

Hijra Arabic for "emigration"; Muhammad's flight from Mecca to Medina in 622 C.E. as a result of anti-Islam hostility. Medina offered to protect Muhammad; he found many willing converts there, and Islam began to thrive. The date of the Hijra marks the beginning of the Islamic calendar.

homage A ritual gesture and ceremony developed in the tenth century in which a new vassal swore his loyalty, trust, and service to a lord. Kneeling, the vassal-to-be first placed his hands between the hands of the lord, vowing to serve him. Then, he swore his allegiance with his hand on relics or a Bible. Such public ceremonies served as visual and verbal contracts in an age when many people could not read or write. *See also* relics; vassalage.

home rule The right demanded by many Catholic Irish to have more say in how they were governed. Home rule was resisted by the British and some Irish (mostly Protestant) residents. Although most of Ireland gained its independence from Britain in 1922, Northern Ireland remained under British control; there, Protestant and Catholic tensions continue to fuel ongoing disputes about where governmental power should lie.

Homo sapiens Latin for "wise" or "clever human being"; the scientific term for humans whose brains and appearances were similar, though not identical, to those of modern people. The earliest known *Homo sapien* remains were found in Ethiopia and have been dated to 160,000 B.C.E., suggesting that *Homo sapiens* first appeared in Africa before migrating to the rest of the world.

hoplite Well-armed soldiers of the Greek infantry. Originating around the eighth century B.C.E., hoplites were citizens who constituted the main strike force of a city-state's militia. The hoplite fought in a phalanx—a solid block of soldiers set up in rows of up to sixteen men that could charge through enemy ranks. A hoplite had to provide his own expensive arms and armor; as such, the hoplite ranks were open only to wealthier citizens. *See also* hoplite revolution.

hoplite revolution A theory put forth by some historians seeking to explain why many Greek city-states extended political rights to poor citizens. The theory hinges on the notion that because of increased prosperity and cheaper weapons after the eighth century B.C.E., more men were able to serve as hoplites but would refuse military participation if not given rights. But this does not account for granting political rights to the poor. A more likely explanation for giving rights to the poor is that they earned respect by fighting as members of light troops to defend their communities, just as the hoplites did. *See also* hoplite.

hubris The Greek term for excessive arrogance, especially when an overconfident human being went against the will of the gods. A popular subject of Greek tragedy, which reached its zenith in the sixth and fifth centuries B.C.E., was the portrayal of characters whose excessive pride over their accomplishments often resulted in catastrophe, usually at the hands of the gods.

Huguenots The name given to Protestants in France in the mid-sixteenth century. A civil war erupted between Huguenots and Catholics in 1562, threatening to destroy the French nation. Mobs killed three thousand Huguenots in the first three days of the St. Bartholomew's Day Massacre in 1572, with ten thousand dying during the next six weeks. These French Wars of Religion paved the way for similar conflicts internationally in subsequent decades. To finally establish control over war-weary France, Henry IV (r. 1589–1610), a Catholic, issued the Edict of Nantes in 1598, granting religious toleration to the roughly 1.2 million Huguenots. *See also* Edict of Nantes.

humanism A literary and intellectual movement that arose in Italy during the early fifteenth century to valorize the writings of Greco-Roman antiquity, such as those of Plato (c. 428–347 B.C.E.) or Cicero (106–43 B.C.E.), and to reconcile classical learning with Christianity. Humanism was so named because its practitioners studied or supported the liberal arts—grammar, rhetoric, poetry, history, and moral philosophy—or humanities. Humanism spread to northern Europe in the late fifteenth and early sixteenth centuries.

humanitas Latin for "humaneness"; a Roman philosophical doctrine stressing generous and honest treatment of others and a commitment to morality based on natural law. Espoused by the orator Cicero (106–43 B.C.E.), humanitas retained its popularity for centuries because of Cicero's fame and greatness. *See also* Stoicism.

humors Vital fluids in the body, which, according to premodern medicine, determined a person's health and mental temperament. Based on ancient medical theory, there were four humors—blood, phlegm, black bile, and yellow bile—each with its own properties and characteristics. Medical practice revolved around keeping these fluids in balance, either by ingesting substances that were believed to have properties similar to the humors or by draining fluids, particularly blood, when there was thought to be an excess.

Hundred Years' War The series of wars (1337–1453) fought intermittently between France and England. Perceived to be one of the most important conflicts in the history of medieval warfare, it began over claims by British kings to the French throne, and after many years of fighting, ultimately resulted in the expulsion of the English from France.

hunter-gatherers People who roamed to find their food in the wild, never settling in one permanent location. Hunter-gatherers such as those during the Paleolithic Age (c. 200,000–10,000 B.C.E.) had not yet learned to farm or raise animals for their nourishment and so subsisted on game, fish, grains, fruits, and nuts. *See also* Paleolithic.

Hussites A religious reform movement based on the preaching of Jan Hus (c. 1373–1415) that took place in Bohemia, a part of the Roman Empire settled by the Czechs. A harsh critic of church corruption, Hus argued against the trafficking of indulgences and the absolution of sin through a cash payment and advocated greater lay participation in the Mass, specifically in the sacrament. Despite a promise of safe passage, he was burned at the stake as a heretic during the Council of Constance (1415), igniting a Bohemian revolution against the Holy Roman Emperor that lasted until 1436.

hygiene The science of maintaining health and cleanliness. During the late nineteenth and early twentieth centuries, hygiene became an increasing part of the day-to-day life of the average citizen. Public hygiene efforts focused on improving sanitation and water quality to prevent the growth and spread of bacteria and disease. The experiments of Louis Pasteur (1822–1895) in the 1850s, for example, advanced this germ theory of disease and revealed that heating foods and liquids such as wine and milk—a process later called pasteurization—killed harmful organisms. Later, personal hygiene emphasized increased bodily cleanliness and led to new consumer products such as deodorant and toothpaste.

I

iconoclasm Greek for "the breaking of icons"; the worship of physical representations of religious figures. Byzantine emperors from 726 to 787 banned icons of Christ, Mary, and the saints and ordered them destroyed. Although icons had been an important feature of seventh-century Byzantine religious life, many people, including the emperor, believed they were prohibited by the Bible's injunction against graven images. A modified ban was revived in 815 and lasted until 843.

idealism A philosophical doctrine established by German Enlightenment thinker Immanuel Kant (1724–1804) in his 1781 book, *The Critique of Pure Reason*. Idealism holds that ideas are shaped not only by sensory information (central to empiricism) but also by framing information in abstract mental categories in the human mind, such as space and time. These "categories of understanding" are neither sensory nor supernatural, meaning that philosophical questions cannot be answered by faith or reason alone. Idealism is one of the foundations of modern philosophy. *See also* empiricism.

ideology A coherent set of beliefs about the way the social and political order should be organized and changed. The word was coined during the French Revolution (1789–1799) to describe the new political and social movements emerging in the late eighteenth and early nineteenth centuries. Prominent ideologies include conservatism, liberalism, and socialism.

IMF *See* International Monetary Fund.

imperialism European dominance of the non-West through economic exploitation and political rule (as distinct from *colonialism*, which usually implies establishment of settler colonies, often with slavery as the labor system); the word was coined in the mid-nineteenth century. Historical examples include France's invasion of Algeria in 1830 and its subsequent imposition of a protectorate government in Tahiti, as well as British annexation of Singapore in 1819 and New Zealand in 1840.

impressionism A mid- to late-nineteenth-century artistic, and later musical, style in which the artist attempted to capture a single moment by focusing on the ever-changing light and color found in ordinary scenes. It derived from Japanese influences and from an opposition to the realism of photographs. Impressionist painters used splotches and dots to convey mood, and musicians likewise looked to re-create a specific atmosphere or mood over narrative and emotions. Notable practitioners included French painter Claude Monet (1840–1926) and French composer Claude Debussy (1862–1918).

Indian National Congress A predominantly Hindu organization dedicated to the rights of Indians and the independence of India from British rule. It was founded in 1885 by educated members of the Indian elite, eventually forming the basis for an independent government when India achieved independence in 1950.

Indian Rebellion of 1857 A revolt led by troops of the Indian army against the expanding British presence in India and Britain's disregard for Indian autonomy and local beliefs. Indian soldiers conquered the old Mogul capital at Delhi and declared independence for India. Known by the British as the Indian Mutiny, the rebellion was quickly put down and led the British to change their governing philosophy in the region. They ended the Mogul Empire, took control of the British East India Company, and implemented a policy of direct rule of India by the British government.

Indo-European The linguistic ancestor of most Mediterranean and European languages, most likely developed between 4500 and 2500 B.C.E. Many languages, including Greek, Latin, and, much later, English, share enough common words and grammatical forms to indicate that they descended from this family of languages.

indulgence In Catholic practice, a remission of sins earned by performing good deeds or religious tasks to avoid purgatory after death. Widely used by the thirteenth century, the practice was based on the Catholic doctrine that Christ had given St. Peter and his successors, the popes, the authority to lift the penalties for sin. The practice eventually developed to include purchasing indulgences for cash, which became a lucrative source of income for the church. This practice came under fire during the Reformation.

Industrial Revolution A series of technological, economic, social, and demographic changes brought about by the introduction of steam-driven machinery, the factory system, and the formation of an urban working class. Also termed *industrialization*, this process of economic transformation began in

Great Britain in the 1770s and 1780s before spreading throughout most of Europe in the first half of the nineteenth century. The Industrial Revolution was characterized by new methods of manufacturing, including machines capable of mass production. They in turn made possible the greater availability and affordability of consumer goods, rapid urbanization, and the rise of a new social class of laborers who worked in urban factories, displacing skilled artisans. Historians also describe a Second Industrial Revolution in the later part of the nineteenth century, which took place primarily in Great Britain and focused on the manufacture of heavy machinery.

infidel A nonbeliever or an outsider with respect to a particular faith. The term is typically used in a hostile sense, depicting infidels as a threat to a religious group, often Christians and Christian leaders in the fifteenth and sixteenth centuries. The artist Michelangelo (1475–1564) became a favorite of Pope Julius II (r. 1503–1513), not only by painting the Sistine Chapel but also by using his artistic talents to glorify a papacy supposedly under siege from infidels.

inflation A continuous and often substantial increase in the price level of goods and services. It is a common feature within capitalism and is often caused by an imbalance between the amount of currency circulating and trade. If currency exceeds trade, inflation results, but it can also be triggered by extra-economic forces, such as the inflation faced by Germany after its defeat in World War I (1914–1918). *See also* capitalism; stagflation.

Inquisition The court of inquiry permanently set up by the Roman Catholic church in 1233. Its purpose was to ferret out and punish heretics and save souls. Inquisitors, aided by secular authorities, rounded up almost entire villages and interrogated everyone, seeking to silence heretics and infidels. Punishments varied; imprisonment—sometimes permanent—was the most common, but the accused also were ordered to go on pilgrimages, were required to wear crosses on their clothes, and occasionally were burned alive.

insulae (singular: insula) Multistory apartment buildings that housed most urban residents in ancient Rome. The first floor of an insula was devoted to small commercial businesses; residents lived in the upper stories, with the wealthy on lower floors, while the less well-off climbed to the higher levels. These buildings often lacked running water and bathrooms; residents carried water up in jugs and were responsible for removing their own trash and waste. Lazy tenants merely tossed it out the window. Sanitation, disease, and crowding posed enormous problems in these apartments and they were in constant danger of collapsing from poor construction.

intelligentsia A Russian term used in the early nineteenth century to designate intellectual and educated elites charged with analyzing the sociopolitical world. Divided into Westerners and Slavophiles, the intelligentsia were nonetheless universally nationalists and ultimately dedicated to revolution. Both Russian leaders V. I. Lenin (1870–1924) and Joseph Stalin (1879–1953) emerged from this class.

intendant A royal official in France who represented the king at the regional level. Unlike other royal officials who traditionally owned and inherited their offices, intendants were appointed by the king; as such, their position was directly linked to serving royal interests. Louis XIV (r. 1643–1715) created the position to enforce his will against the entrenched local interests of parlements, noble governors, and provincial estates.

International Monetary Fund (IMF) An organization founded at the United Nations Monetary and Financial Conference in Bretton Woods, New Hampshire, in 1944 toward the end of World War II (1939–1945). Attended by representatives of forty-four nations, the meeting sought to ensure monetary stability through the maintenance of international financial cooperation and the stabilization of exchange rates. With funds raised from international governments, the IMF made loans in the 1990s to developing countries on the condition that they restructure their economies according to neoliberal principles. *See also* neoliberalism.

Investiture Conflict The confrontation between Pope Gregory VII (r. 1073–1085) and Holy Roman Emperor Henry IV (r. 1056–1106) over the right to appoint and install bishops. Each man believed that his office entitled him to lead the church and make all appointments. The struggle between Gregory and Henry led to intermittent war from 1077 to 1122, ultimately ending the secular leader's role in choosing churchmen and setting the wheels in motion for the modern distinction between church and state.

Irish Christianity The unique type of Christianity that emerged in early medieval Ireland after that country's conversion in the fifth century C.E. by St. Patrick and other missionaries. This form of Christianity was structured around the rural clan and centered around the monastery rather than the city. Irish Christians found themselves at odds with the Roman church, which stressed the centrality of the pope and the organization of the church under bishops rather than the Irish system of abbots. They also differed over the calculation of the date of Easter, and each celebrated on a different day.

Irish famine A period from 1845 to 1849 during which the failure of Ireland's staple potato crops caused widespread famine and death and fueled a massive immigration to the United States. Also known as the Great Hunger, up to one million people died and another million and a half emigrated. The population of Ireland never returned to prefamine levels.

"iron and blood" An important speech given by the Prussian prime minister Otto von Bismarck (1815–1898) in 1862. It outlined the shift in Prussian governance from a liberal viewpoint to a more aggressive, militarized philosophy that sought to limit civilian control of the military, as had been advocated by liberals in government to the dismay of Emperor William I. Noting this shift and his mission to rebuild the army under government control, von Bismarck stated, "The great questions of the day will not be settled by means of speeches and majority decisions . . . but by iron and blood."

isonomia The Greek term for equality under the law. Originally proposed during the reforms of Cleisthenes (r. c. 600–c. 570 B.C.E.) in 500 B.C.E., the concept of isonomia by 460 had become a reality and ensured that elites were not the only members of juries. Politicians such as Pericles (c. 495–429 B.C.E.) championed isonomia in part to gain wider political support.

J

Jacobin Club An influential political club formed at the beginning of the French Revolution (1789–1799). Named for the former monastery in Paris where the club first met, the Jacobins established a nationwide network of affiliated groups and provided much of the leadership during the Revolution, particularly during the Terror. They divided into two factions after the fall of the monarchy in 1792: the Girondins, who were opposed to the execution of the king, and the Mountain, which was allied with the increasingly powerful Parisian militants who favored the execution of the king. *See also* Girondins; Mountain; Terror.

Jacobitism From the Latin *Jacobus* for "James"; the movement of support for deposed British king James II (r. 1685–1688) in the early eighteenth century. Prominent in Ireland and Scotland, Jacobitism led to the Act of Union in 1707, which dissolved the Scottish Parliament and brought Scotland under the direct control of the British Parliament, which in turn began to include Scottish members.

Jacquerie uprising A revolt of the peasantry in Paris, France, in 1358 against the abuses of the privileged classes. In particular, the rebellion was fueled by popular discontent over the heavy taxes raised to finance the Hundred Years' War (1337–1453), the incompetence of the nobility, and roving bands of mercenary soldiers who victimized the peasantry in the countryside. The insurgents destroyed castles, stole provisions, and committed other acts of violence before the uprising was brutally suppressed with thousands of rebels killed in battle or executed. The name comes from both *jacque*, the jacket worn by serfs, and *Jacques Bonhomme*, a contemporary nickname for French peasants, translated as "simple Jack."

Janissaries Christian slave children and war captives who were raised by the Ottoman sultan as Muslims and served in the army from the fourteenth to the nineteenth century. An elite military unit, they trained under strict codes of discipline and ultimately gained power within the Ottoman Empire (Turkey). The rank of Janissary was so desirable that by the seventeenth century, membership was only through inheritance, although some Muslims did attempt to join by bribery.

Jansenism A religious movement among French Catholics that embraced predestination and denied the presence of free will. Based on the writings of Flemish theologian Cornelius Jansen (1585–1638), Jansenists resembled English Puritans in their emphasis on an austere lifestyle, concern with original sin, and belief that only through God's grace was salvation possible. It had great appeal among members of the parlements and conservative urban elites. Although suppressed by Louis XIV (r. 1643–1715) in 1660, Jansenism experienced a resurgence in the 1720s and was part of the wider movement of religious revival experienced in Europe in the early eighteenth century.

Jesuits *See* Society of Jesus.

June Days Part of the Revolution of 1848 in France; a rebellion by French workers who had grown disgruntled when they found their dreams of reform would not be met. The actual spark happened days before when the government ordered national workshops closed to new workers and told those already employed to join the army. Beginning June 24 and lasting a week, tens of thousands of workers took to the streets against the government, which called in the National Guard to squash the upheaval. Ten thousand rebels, most of them workers, were killed or wounded; another twelve thousand were arrested; and four thousand rebels were later convicted and deported. The violence of the June Days led the Constituent Assembly to strengthen the power of the executive branch, which set the stage for the emergence of Louis Napoleon Bonaparte (1808–1873) as leader of the state.

Junkers The landed aristocracy (nobles) in Brandenburg-Prussia. The Junkers had a great deal of autonomy over their enserfed peasants—workers bound by heredity to the manor in a kind of semibondage—granted by Frederick William (r. 1640–1688) in exchange for the right to collect taxes. The Junkers were a barrier to Frederick II's (r. 1740–1786) attempts at reform in the eighteenth century and as a class continued to exert a dominant conservative force on Prussian and German society well into the twentieth century.

K

khagan Literally, "khan of khans"; the ruler in charge of all the Mongol peoples. A concentrated Mongol assault on Germany was only prevented by the death of the khagan Ogodei in 1241.

Kievan Russia The kingdom established by the Vikings in Russia in the ninth century. Arriving from the north, the Vikings originally ruled over the native Slavic population of Russia but gradually blended in with them. By the end of the century, the chief ruler, Oleg, extended his reach into southwestern Russia, including the thriving commercial city of Kiev, which became the nucleus for the tribal association he created there. Kievan Russia had extensive contact with the Byzantine world, which ultimately resulted in Russian conversion to Byzantine Christianity and adoption of the Cyrillic alphabet. *See also* Vikings.

Koine The common or shared form of the Greek language that spread to become the international language in the Hellenistic period (c. 323–30 B.C.E.). It facilitated commerce, cultural exchange, and the transmission of ideas throughout much of Alexander the Great's (r. 336–323 B.C.E.) former empire.

Kristallnacht German for "crystal night"; the evening of November 9, 1938, when the Nazis staged a concerted attack on Jews and their property in Germany and its territories. Incited by a radio speech by Nazi propaganda minister Joseph Goebbels (1897–1945), rioters burned and looted Jewish businesses, synagogues, and homes, killing 91 Jews and destroying over 7,500 businesses. The Nazi government then fined the Jewish community and ordered them to pay for the damage incurred during the riot. The "Night of Broken Glass" came to symbolize the virulent anti-Semitism of the Nazi state. *See also* anti-Semitism.

kulak Russian for "fist"; used by the communists during the 1917 October Revolution, also known as the Russian Revolution, to describe the prosperous landed peasants as exploiters of the poor. V. I. Lenin's (1870–1924) "crusade for bread" in 1918 advocated that the Bolshevik government begin confiscating the grain produced by these farmers to feed starving workers. By the late 1920s, communists began evicting landed peasants and taking their grain; these measures were formalized when

Joseph Stalin (1879–1953) began a broader campaign to end private farms in favor of cooperative ones. *See also* Bolshevik.

Kulturkampf German for "culture war"; in the 1870s, a reference to German chancellor Otto von Bismarck's (1815–1898) attempt to fight the cultural power of the church through a series of injurious policies. The government expelled the Jesuit order from Germany in 1872, increased state power over the clergy in 1873, and made civil marriage legally required in 1875. Both conservatives and Catholics rebelled against policies of religious repression as state building, and competition between church and state intensified.

L

labor-intensive industry A business that relies heavily on workers rather than on machinery or capital. Typical examples include agriculture, mining, and service businesses. *See also* capital-intensive industry.

ladder of offices A series of elective government offices Romans had to climb in the early republic (beginning c. 287) to gain the consulship. The first step required military service of approximately ten years. Then came election to the offices of quaestor, aedile, praetor, and finally consul.

laissez-faire French for "leave it alone"; an economic doctrine that advocates freeing economies from government intervention and control. Developed by British economist Adam Smith in his work *An Inquiry into the Nature and Causes of the Wealth of Nations* (1776), this ideology resulted from the application of Enlightenment principles of individual liberty to economics. Smith insisted governments eliminate all restrictions on the sale of land, remove restraints on grain trade, and abandon duties on imports. He believed that free international trade would stimulate growth worldwide and therefore enhance national wealth.

lares Roman statuettes depicting ancestral spirits that comprised part of a household shrine. The spirits were believed to keep the family well and maintain moral traditions. *See also* penates.

lateen sail A triangular-shaped sail that gives a ship greater maneuverability in varying wind directions. Although in use for thousands of years in the Indian Ocean and the Arab world, this type of sale was adopted in western Europe only in the late Middle Ages. This technology allowed European ships to sail the Atlantic Ocean and facilitated the voyages of discovery in the fifteenth and sixteenth centuries.

latifundia Rich landowners' huge farms worked by gangs of slaves. The term is most commonly used in reference to the Roman plantations that developed after the Punic Wars (262–241 B.C.E., 218–201 B.C.E., and 149–146 B.C.E.).

law of universal gravitation Scientist Sir Isaac Newton's (1642–1727) attempt to explain the most baffling question of seventeenth-century science: how the planets and other celestial bodies move in a systematic and orderly manner. Influenced by the work of Italian scientist Galileo (1564–1642), Newton argued in his groundbreaking *Principia Mathematica* (1687) that mutual attraction—or gravity—explained all movement, from planetary orbits to an apple falling on the ground. While he never discussed the nature of gravity itself, his law of universal gravitation gained prestige for the field of science in the late seventeenth and early eighteenth centuries and became the basis for the study of physics for generations.

League of Nations The international organization set up following World War I (1914–1918) to maintain peace by arbitrating disputes and promoting collective security. It was ultimately an ineffectual body, hampered by, among other things, the United States' lack of participation, despite the fact that the league had been President Woodrow Wilson's (1913–1921) vision.

Lebensraum German for "living space"; a belief that emerged in the early twentieth century that held that Germany needed space for the expansion of its peoples and culture. It also came to represent the land that Adolf Hitler (1889–1945) proposed to conquer so that true Aryans might have sufficient space to live their noble lives.

legion A Roman military unit of five thousand soldiers. Stationed throughout the empire, Roman legions were responsible for defending the borders and providing security within the Roman world.

Levellers Disgruntled lower-class soldiers in Oliver Cromwell's (1599–1658) New Model Army who wanted to "level" social differences and extend political participation to all male property owners. They saw in the English Civil War in the mid-seventeenth century an opportunity to reform British society; however, they were brutally suppressed by Cromwell's government.

liberalism An early nineteenth-century economic and political ideology that emphasized free trade and individual rights such as freedom of speech and religion as the best means for promoting social and economic improvement. Liberalism traces its origins to the writings of John Locke (1632–1704); it was also influenced by the Enlightenment. Liberals favored the social and economic changes brought about by the Industrial Revolution but disapproved of the violence and excessive state power promoted by the French Revolution (1789–1799). *See also* Enlightenment; ideology.

limited liability corporation A legal entity developed in mid- to late-nineteenth-century Germany, and later in the United States, that protected a company's investors from being personally responsible for the firm's financial obligations. It limited an investor's risk and responsibility to the size of the investment and ultimately held that only the business's assets—and not those belonging privately to the owner—could be sold to cover debts in case of financial failure. This practice has become the hallmark of Western business structure.

Linear B The Mycenaean pictographic script (c. 1800–1300 B.C.E.) considered the earliest known form of written Greek. It was used primarily for administrative purposes and record keeping.

lithograph A mass-produced print using an inked stone. Lithographs played a key role in social commentary and political discussion in the 1830s through the 1850s. Artists used them to publish their critiques in newspapers, where they reached and enlightened a mass audience. In the early to mid-nineteenth century, the French artist Honoré Daumier published four thousand prints and caricatures criticizing the inequalities created by economic development.

Lombard Italy Parts of Italy under the rule of the Lombard family from the 570s until Charlemagne's (r. 768–814 C.E.) conquest of the peninsula in 774. Originally Arian Christians, the Lombards converted only gradually to Catholic Christianity. Consequently, they never won the support of important churchmen and remained rivals with the papacy in Rome. *See also* Arianism.

lycées State-run secondary schools for boys established in France under Napoleon I (r. 1804–1814) in the early nineteenth century. Designed to shape young men into citizens, these schools required boys to wear uniforms, and drum rolls signaled the beginning and end of class sessions. One of the many enduring legacies of the Napoleonic era, the lycées are the basis of the modern French educational system, though without the military flourishes.

lyric poetry Greek poetry sung with the accompaniment of the lyre, a small stringed instrument. Based on Near Eastern verse, lyric poems, first developed in the Archaic Age (c. 650–500 B.C.E.), covered a range of subjects. Some praised victorious athletes or honored deities, others celebrated emotions such as love.

M

Maastricht Treaty The agreement among the members of the European Community to establish a closer alliance that would ideally prove economically beneficial, including the use of common passports and the development of a common currency. Under the terms of this treaty, the European Community became the European Union (EU) in 1994. *See also* euro; European Economic Community (EEC); European Union (EU).

Maat Egyptian goddess who stood for truth, justice, and cosmic order. In the Egyptian Old Kingdom (c. 3050–2190 B.C.E.), the king's rule was considered divine, but he was expected to operate according to Maat's principles, namely, promoting law and keeping the forces of nature in balance.

machine gun A weapon that fires multiple rounds of ammunition per minute without reloading. The first automatic machine gun was the Maxim gun, invented in England in the mid-1880s, although hand-powered automatic rifles, such as the Gatling gun, were widely used as early as the American Civil War (1861–1865). The machine gun became an important tool of European imperialism from the late nineteenth century forward and significantly changed the nature of warfare beginning with World War I (1914–1918).

madrasa Islamic school located within or attached to a mosque. Often founded by a wealthy Muslim as a demonstration of his piety and charity, the madrasa was a key feature of the Islamic Renaissance (c. 790–1050 C.E.). The all-male student body chose from classes about the Qur'an and other literary or legal texts. Most students paid tuition, but scholarships were available for the needy.

Magna Carta The document signed by King John (r. 1199–1216) in 1215 that granted English barons and churchmen specific rights and privileges as "free men." Considered a landmark of constitutional government, "the Great Charter," as it was known, was an attempt to correct perceived abuses by the king and safeguard against a recurrence in the future. It set forth rights and customs that the king was required to observe and allowed the king's subjects to declare war against him if he failed in his duties. The term *free men* originally referred to the nobility but, over time, became a guarantee to all Englishmen.

Magyars A nomadic people who arrived in Europe from the east around 899, establishing themselves in present-day Hungary. The Magyars raided as far west as Gaul and Italy until their defeat at the Battle of Lechfeld in 955 by the German king Otto I (r. 936–973 C.E.).

mamluks Mercenary soldiers, typically Turkish slaves or freemen. Mamluks were often recruited and employed by Islamic rulers to stave off power struggles following the death in 809 of Harun al-Rashid, the fifth and most famous Abbasid caliph ruler, whose empire ultimately included Southwest Asia and most of Africa. Mamluks were well paid, and many later gained high positions at the courts of the rulers they defended. *See also* Abbasid; caliphs.

mandate system The League of Nations covenant that granted the victors of World War I (1914–1918) in its membership— chiefly Britain and France, as well as South Africa, New Zealand, Australia, and Japan—political control over Germany's former colonies, such as Togo, Cameroon, Syria, and Palestine. It continued the practice of carving up the globe into territories controlled by various European powers at a time when many of those countries were themselves weak and bankrupt. The mandate system aroused anger and resistance both in the territories and among German citizens.

mannerism A late-sixteenth-century painting style in which a distorted perspective created bizarre and theatrical effects that contrasted with the precise, harmonious lines of Renaissance painting. Emerging in the Italian states and best exemplified in the paintings of El Greco (1541–1614), mannerism sought to achieve an emotional intensity. It is closely associated with the Catholic Reformation because faith and religious fervor were often key motivators for these artists.

manor A large, organized estate consisting normally of arable fields, vineyards, meadows, and woodland, ordinarily owned by a lord or religious body. A key financial institution of the Carolingian era (c. 750–900), manors did not rely on slave labor as in Roman times, but rather on peasant families who were provided their own homes, gardens, and small plots of land to farm. Carolingian manors never produced great surpluses; consequently, dependence on them proved a source of weakness.

manuscript illuminations Painted illustrations or embellishments in hand-copied manuscripts, often gospels. Manuscript illuminations represent the merging of classical and Christian traditions; medieval monks often based their work on early Greek illuminations. They also drew on traditional imagery so that their subjects would be easily understood and identifiable. The Lindisfarne Gospels, illuminated by monks on the British Isle of Lindisfarne, were elaborately decorated with fanciful letters, embellished carpet motifs surrounding the text, and even portraits of evangelists.

march on Rome   The threat by Benito Mussolini (1883–1945) and his followers in 1922 to take over the Italian government in a military convergence on Rome. The march forced the Italian king Victor Emmanuel III (r. 1900–1946) to make Mussolini prime minister.

Marshall Plan   A post–World War II loan program funded by the United States to get Europe back on its feet economically and thereby reduce the appeal and threat of communism. It played an important role in the rebirth of European prosperity in the 1950s.

martyr   Greek for "witness"; a person who dies for his or her religious beliefs. The persecutions of the early Christians (c. 64–313 C.E.) in the Roman world resulted in many martyrs, some of whom accepted their fate because they believed they would be rewarded in heaven.

Marxism   An economic and political philosophy concerning the organization of production, social inequality, and the processes of revolutionary change as devised by the philosopher and economist Karl Marx (1818–1883) in the mid- to late nineteenth century. It was at the core of most socialist and communist political theories and became central, at least in name, to the economic foundation of the Soviet Union as oppositional to capitalism. *See also* capitalism; communism.

mass culture   Also known as "popular culture"; artistic materials designed for and circulated to the widest possible audience, often via mass media (movies, advertisements, radio, television, and more recently, the Internet). Critics have often argued that mass culture waters down art, stripping it of its deeper and intended meaning by reducing it to an easily accessible form.

materialism   The philosophical doctrine that stresses that only things made of matter truly exist. Hellenistic philosophers (c. 323–30 B.C.E.) stressed materialism, which denied Plato's concept of a soul and all other nonmaterial phenomena. Materialism greatly influenced Roman thinkers and, subsequently, many important Western philosophers who read classical texts. *See also* metaphysics.

mean Aristotle's term for striking a balance between suppressing and overindulging in physical yearnings to live a just and worthwhile life. Aristotle (384–322 B.C.E.) believed in cultivating self-control and stressed the power of the human mind in governing the body.

medieval According to some historians, the time period from 600 to 1400 C.E. Considered derogatory, the term was first used in the sixteenth century by Renaissance scholars to distinguish their period as far more advanced than what they termed the more barbaric and ignorant world of the classical Greeks and Romans. In the nineteenth century, historians divided this time period into three distinct ages, again signifying that some parts marked higher development than others: early Middle Ages (c. 600–1100), high Middle Ages (c. 1100–1300), and late Middle Ages (c. 1300–1400). Today, however, historians categorize the Middle Ages as marked by a variety of peoples, informal methods of government, and community involvement.

Mediterranean polyculture A method of farming in which olives, grapes, and grains are all cultivated in a single, interrelated system. Emerging during the Minoan civilization (c. 2200–1400 B.C.E.), it later became the dominant form of Mediterranean agriculture. It is significant because it provided a healthy diet and stimulated the production of valuable goods, such as wine and olive oil.

Meiji Restoration From Japanese for "enlightened rule"; a change in the Japanese government in 1867 that reinstalled the emperor as legitimate ruler in place of the military leader, or shogun, who had ruled for two centuries. The goal of the Meiji Restoration was to establish Japan as a modern, technologically powerful state free from Western control. It inspired other regions in Asia and Africa to similarly resist the West.

mendicants Members of a religious order who take a vow of poverty and depend on the charity of others. *See also* friars; tertiaries.

mercantilism The doctrine that governments should intervene to increase national wealth by any means, such as establishing overseas trading companies, granting manufacturing monopolies, and standardizing production methods. Developed by Louis XIV (r. 1643–1715) of France's finance minister Jean-Baptiste Colbert in the second half of the seventeenth century, mercantilism was adopted in many European states and contributed to the expansion of state bureaucracies.

mercenary A soldier for hire who fights for wages, as opposed to fighting for feudal obligations or to defend his homeland. Mercenaries supplemented armies in ancient Persia and Greece, in Rome, and in Byzantium. In fourteenth-century Europe, the Black Death caused nobles, who traditionally had comprised the warrior class and lived off the profits of the land they owned, to seek new sources of revenue as food prices plummeted and income from their land declined. Mercenaries figured prominently in the Hundred Years' War (1337–1453) between France and England. The use of mercenaries represented an important shift in the nature of warfare, as commoners and criminals replaced knights and their chivalric combat. *See also* Black Death; chivalry.

Merovingian dynasty The family of rulers who were the first kings of the Frankish people. The Merovingian dynasty lasted from 486 to 751 C.E. and endured by allying with local lay aristocrats and ecclesiastical authorities. Kings enhanced their power by acting as intermediaries for aristocratic conflict. Rarely did the Franks have only one king, and by the seventh century three relatively cohesive Frankish kingdoms had emerged in Austrasia, Neustria, and Burgundy.

mestizo A person of mixed ancestry in the Spanish colonies, typically descended from a European father and a Native American mother. By 1800 mestizos accounted for more than a quarter of the colonial population, with many aspiring to join the local elite.

metaphysics Ideas about the ultimate nature of reality beyond the reach of human senses. Metaphysics was an intellectual interest of the Greek philosopher Plato (429–348 B.C.E.), who argued for the existence of an invisible and imperceptible soul. *See also* materialism.

Methodism An offshoot of Anglicanism that appeared in England in the late eighteenth century and insisted on strict self-discipline and a "methodical" approach to religious study and observance. Founded by John Wesley (1703–1791), whose followers were also called Wesleyans, Methodism stressed individual religious experience over reason as the true path to social and moral reform. Although politically conservative in many regards, Methodism was more liberal in its disdain for rigid religious doctrine and its encouragement of popular preaching, even by women.

metic A foreigner granted permanent residence in a Greek city-state in exchange for obligations to pay taxes and serve in the military. The work of the metics contributed greatly to Athens's prosperous Golden Age (c. 500–400 B.C.E.), yet they remained outsiders in terms of political rights and were not allowed to vote.

millennialism An idea deriving from Judeo-Christian theology that a Golden Age on Earth will last for one thousand years prior to the end of the world and final judgment. During this Golden Age, it was believed that great joy and prosperity would prevail. Millennial ideas have existed throughout the last two thousand years, rising and fading according to other social phenomena. Millennialism reemerged, for example, following the development of nuclear weapons in the mid-twentieth century.

mir A Russian farm community fortified by the emancipation of the serfs in 1861 that provided for holding the land in common and regulating the movements of any individual by the group. The mir hindered the free movement of labor and individual agricultural enterprise, including modernization.

missi dominici Latin for "those sent out by the lord king"; special officials, often bishops and lay aristocrats, used by Charlemagne (r. 768–814 C.E.) to oversee regional governors and discourage corruption. The missi dominici traveled in pairs to make a circuit of regions in the kingdom, investigating claims of injustice and attempting to bring law to the entire Carolingian world.

missionary An individual working as an agent of Christianity to ultimately convert nonbelievers, often in undeveloped or underdeveloped areas of the world. Missionaries do charitable work in foreign countries, building schools and aiding in farming and other needs, while hoping to Christianize and "save the souls" of those they assist. Missionaries were sent to Mexico and other areas explored by Europeans in the sixteenth century. In the nineteenth and twentieth centuries, they traveled to areas claimed by Europe in Africa, South Asia, China, and South America.

Mitteleuropa German for "central Europe"; used by influential military leaders in Germany before World War I (1914–1918) to refer to land in central and eastern Europe that they hoped to acquire as a substitute for vast colonial empires in Africa and Asia. This territory ultimately formed a war aim in World War I and for Adolf Hilter (1889–1945) thereafter.

modernism An artistic movement at the end of the nineteenth century that featured a break with realism in art and literature and with lyricism in music. Encompassing a wide variety of styles and approaches, the modernist movement broke with traditional styles and accepted artistic forms. It continued through the twentieth century and included the work of such disparate artists as French painter Edouard Manet (1832–1883) (considered its first practitioner), English novelist Virginia Woolf (1882–1941), and Dutch painter Piet Mondrian (1872–1944).

monasticism From the Greek *monos*, meaning "single" or "solitary"; a movement within Christian asceticism emphasizing the retreat from the everyday world to live a life of self-denial and prayer. Monasticism first emerged in Egypt in the second half of the third century but soon spread throughout the European and Mediterranean worlds. Known as monks, practitioners originally lived alone but gradually formed communities providing mutual support in the pursuit of holiness.

Mongols Nomadic tribes from the grassy steppes of central Asia who expanded westward into Russia, Poland, and Hungary and eastward into China under the leadership of Genghis Khan (c. 1162–1227) and his sons. They collected tribute, or taxes in exchange for protection, from Russia for nearly two hundred years, and the effort to expel the Mongols led to the organization of a consolidated Russian state in the fifteenth century. The Mongols also brought Europe closer to the Far East by reopening land routes and encouraging trade relationships.

monophysitism The Christian doctrine that holds that Jesus did not have separate divine and human natures, but rather a single divine nature. Followers of monophysitism split with the orthodox hierarchy on this issue in the sixth century and founded churches in Egypt (the Coptic church), Ethiopia, Syria, and Armenia.

monotheism Greek for "single-natured belief"; the belief in the existence of only one God, a characteristic of Christianity, Judaism, and Islam. The Pharaoh Akhenaten (r. 1375–1355 B.C.E.), who forced the Egyptian people to worship a single deity named Aten, is believed by some historians to have been the first monotheist. *See also* polytheism.

Moors Muslims who lived under Christian rule in Spain and Portugal in the mid-fourteenth century. After the fall of Granada in 1492, the Moors were given the choice of conversion to Christianity or expulsion from the country.

moral dualism The perception that the world is the arena for an ongoing struggle between the opposing divine forces of good and evil. A key tenet of the Persian Zoroastrian religion (founded c. 1200–1000 B.C.E.), it stressed that human beings would have to choose between the way of the truth and the way of the lie, and only those deemed righteous after death would be welcomed in heaven.

Moriscos The Spanish term for Muslims who had converted to Christianity in lieu of exile after the fall of Granada in 1492. Many of the so-called converts were believed to remain secretly faithful to Islam. After the Morisco revolt in southern Spain between 1568 and 1570, Philip III (r. 1598–1621) ordered their expulsion in 1614.

motet From the French *mot*, meaning "word"; the most distinctive musical form of the thirteenth century. Originating in Paris, the motet is a two- or three-part polyphonic song that weaves together sacred Latin church melodies with secular French text. Motets were written by and for a clerical elite but incorporated the music of the ordinary people. *See also* polyphony.

Mountain A political party that emerged during the French Revolution (1789–1799) after the fall of the monarchy in 1792; one faction of the Jacobins. The Mountain, which got its name from the fact that its deputies occupied the highest seats in the National Convention, was closely allied with Parisian militants and favored the execution of Louis XVI (r. 1774–1792) for treason. The Mountain's conflict with the Girondins was one of the main factors leading to the Terror. *See also* Girondins; Jacobin Club; Terror.

movable type A printing technology in which reusable individual letters are set in a frame to create blocks of text that are then pressed onto a page. This mechanical printing was a dramatic improvement over earlier, expensive, and time-consuming methods, either copying by hand or carving an entire page onto a single wooden block. Johannes Gutenberg, a German goldsmith (c. 1400–1470), is generally credited with developing movable type in Europe in the 1440s; it was initially developed in China before the early thirteenth century but abandoned because it did not work well with the expansive Chinese alphabet.

Movable type and the printing press represent one of the greatest technological achievements in the West because they made mass production of books and written materials possible and therefore made books and knowledge available to wide audiences. This in turn facilitated the circulation of scientific and technological advances and the exchange of new ideas.

multinational corporation A business that operates in many foreign countries by sending large segments of its manufacturing, finance, sales, and other business components abroad. Beginning in the early twentieth century and expanding dramatically after World War II (1931–1945), they have taken on increased importance in the late twentieth century with the rise of the global economy. Most multinational corporations are based in their home country—typically Japan, the United States, or a western European country—but manufacture abroad, often in third world countries where labor costs are inexpensive. These companies also wield great influence in their home countries and across the globe.

mystery cult A religious group whose secret rites involved prayers, hymns, ritual purification, sacrifices, and other forms of worship. Popular during the Golden Age of Athens (c. 500–400 B.C.E.), mystery cults were connected with individual deities and centered on providing worshippers with divine protection and secret knowledge about the celestial and human worlds.

mysticism Religious practices that emphasize a personal, internal, emotional connection with God as more important than external, formal religious behavior. All world religions have had mystical movements, which were occasionally regarded with suspicion by religious authorities.

N

NAFTA *See* North American Free Trade Agreement.

nation-state A sovereign political entity of modern times representing a united people instead of a collection of disparate cities or regions. Examples of nation-states include Italy, Germany, and the United States.

nationalism A political ideology that holds that all people derive their identities from their nations, which are defined by a shared language, history, customs, and traditions. Emerging in the West in the early nineteenth century, nationalism was influenced by romanticism and resistance to Napoleonic rule and posed a serious challenge to the rule of multiethnic empires such as the Ottoman Empire and the Austrian Empire. Nationalist competition helped fuel imperialism in the late nineteenth century and the world wars of the twentieth century. It continues to be a source of tension and conflict throughout the world. For example, nationalism has intensified since the breakup of the Soviet Union, the crisis and fall of Yugoslavia, and the growth of Muslim fundamentalism. *See also* imperialism.

NATO *See* North Atlantic Treaty Organization.

natural law/natural rights A legal theory in which certain laws are inherent in the order of nature itself and are independent from, and above, political or divine authority. The concept of natural law existed in the Middle Ages and held that moral standards were founded on nature rather than social custom or convention. In the early seventeenth century, legal scholars such as Hugo Grotius (1583–1645) adapted the concept of natural law to argue that nature endowed people with certain rights, namely life, body, freedom, and honor, which governments were bound to uphold. This new concept of natural rights and natural law played an important role in the founding of constitutional governments from the mid-seventeenth century forward.

Nazi-Soviet Pact The agreement reached in 1939 by Germany and the Soviet Union in which both agreed not to attack the other in case of war. The agreement secretly divided up territory that would later be conquered and made it possible for Germany to avoid fighting a war on two fronts. The pact fell apart when Adolf Hitler (1889–1945) invaded Russia in 1941.

neoclassicism An artistic movement of the seventeenth and eighteenth centuries that emphasized order and a rational clarity of forms in stark contrast to the emotion and asymmetry of the baroque and rococo styles. Using designs inspired by newly discovered Greek and Roman archaeological sites in Italy, the neoclassical style was also driven by middle-class desires to emulate the wealthy. *See also* baroque; rococo.

neoliberalism A theory promoted by British prime minister Margaret Thatcher (r. 1979–1990) and her followers calling for a return to nineteenth-century liberal principles, including the reduction of welfare-state programs and the cutting of taxes for wealthy people to promote economic growth. Initially, her program met with much public disapproval, as the quality of universities, public transportation, and medical care deteriorated. Only after Thatcher declared war with Argentina in 1982 did the economy stabilize. While historians debate whether it was her policy or the war that brought results, her program nonetheless became the standard.

Neolithic Literally, "New Stone"; the second period of the Stone Age (c. 10,000–4000 B.C.E.). The Neolithic era is noted for the development of farming and domesticated animals on which modern societies would come to depend, as well as the creation of elaborate tools, weapons, and jewelry. *See also* Paleolithic.

Neolithic Revolution A term used by historians to describe the changes in human life resulting from the development of agricultural production and the domestication of animals during the New Stone Age (beginning 10,000–8000 B.C.E.). The Neolithic Revolution marked the birth of modern life, as formerly nomadic people settled in areas with fertile land and adequate water supplies and supported themselves from farming rather than roaming in search of food. *See also* Neolithic.

Neoplatonism Spiritual philosophy based on the teachings of Plato (429–348 B.C.E.), developed by the Roman Plotinus (c. 205–270 C.E.). Embraced by educated Christians and polytheists, Neoplatonism focused on human longing to return to the universal good from which all human existence derives. It emphasized spiritual purity through self-discipline and intellectual pursuits.

Nestorianism The Christian doctrine that held that Jesus was born human but later became divine. This doctrine was originally promulgated by Nestorius, named bishop of Constantinople in 428. Condemned by the orthodox hierarchy, his followers, the Nestorians, formed a new church in Persia that flourished until 1300.

new man A Roman man who was the first in his family to serve as consul. New men emerged in the second century B.C.E. in response to crises in military and political leadership. Although not from established noble families, their successful military endeavors allowed new men to enter the highest political office. The general Gaius Marius (c. 157–86 B.C.E.), who earned victories in North Africa, southern France, and Italy, was a new man who was elected consul an unprecedented six times.

nihilism From the Latin meaning "nothing"; a skeptical philosophy emerging in Russia in the 1860s whose adherents claim to believe in nothing (especially regarding social and political values). In its most radical form, it also suggests that nothing can be known and all life is meaningless. The term is associated with the nineteenth-century German philosopher Friedrich Nietzsche (1844–1900) and the existentialist movement in the twentieth century. *See also* existentialism.

nobility of the robe A new social elite in France that emerged in the sixteenth century. It was comprised of wealthy merchants and lawyers who purchased offices from the king that, in turn, conferred nobility on their holders. These robe nobles, so called because of the magisterial garments they wore, were distinct from the "nobility of the sword," or the traditional aristocracy whose status was based on military service. The sale of titles of nobility created a new revenue stream that provided a foundation for a strong monarchy and absolutism.

nominalism A late medieval philosophy that held that universal concepts, such as "man" or "papal infallibility," have no reality in nature but exist only as representations, or merely as words. Nominalists argued that observation and human reason were the only ways to understand the universe and know God. Nominalists contrasted with earlier Aristotelian philosophers, such as Thomas Aquinas (1225–1274), who believed that mental concepts and ideas did indeed have a real existence in nature.

nongovernmental organizations (NGOs) Charitable foundations and activist groups such as Doctors Without Borders that often work internationally on political, economic, and relief issues, shaping policies and the course of political reform.

Normans Viking people who settled in the northwest region of France known as Normandy in the late ninth century C.E.

The Normans, led by Duke William (later called William the Conqueror), invaded England after the death of the English king Edward the Confessor (r. 1042–1066). William's victory at Hastings gave the English crown to the Norman people. The resulting kings of England would own considerable land in France, exacerbating the tense relations between the two kingdoms. *See also* Vikings.

North American Free Trade Agreement (NAFTA) A 1994 treaty that established a free-trade zone between the United States, Mexico, and Canada by providing for the elimination of tariffs and other economic barriers. Its intent was to encourage economic growth and raise the standard of living in these regions, especially as European nations began to ally economically under the rubric of the European Union (EU). *See also* European Union (EU).

North Atlantic Treaty Organization (NATO) The security alliance formed in 1949 to provide a unified military force for the United States, Canada, and their allies in western Europe and Scandinavia. The corresponding alliance of the Soviet Union and its allies was known as the Warsaw Pact. *See also* Warsaw Pact.

Northwest Passage A hypothetical, but much hoped for, shortcut route between the Atlantic and Pacific oceans through the Arctic region of northern Canada. Such a passage would have dramatically reduced the ocean voyage between Europe and the Far East, and the search for it motivated much of the exploration of the North American coastline in the sixteenth century.

Nuremberg A city in Germany that was heavily bombed in World War II (1939–1945). It became the site of the famous war crimes tribunals after the war, where the remaining Nazi leadership was put on trial between 1945 and 1946 for crimes against humanity.

Nuremberg Laws Legislation in 1935 that deprived Jewish Germans of their citizenship and imposed many other hardships on them, such as forbidding marriage between Jews and non-Jews. These laws were part of a broader Nazi racial policy of discrimination against so-called non-Aryans, specifically Jews.

O

Old Believers A Russian Orthodox religious group in the mid-seventeenth century that rejected state efforts to modernize the Russian church and bring Russian worship in line with Byzantine tradition. Many Old Believers were imprisoned or exiled, and some killed themselves rather than submit to the changes.

OPEC *See* Organization of Petroleum Exporting Countries.

opium An addictive drug derived from the heads of poppy plants. Opium was imported to Europe from the Ottoman Empire and India, was available in various forms, and was often used by ordinary people as a medicinal treatment or for recreation. Though its use was restricted in 1868, it remained easily available until the twentieth century. Writers and artists sometimes glamorized the drug, believing it enhanced their creativity.

optimates A Roman political faction supporting the "best" or highest (often their own) social class rather than siding with supporters of the people (*populares*). The upper class became increasingly divided following the death of Gaius Gracchus in 121 B.C.E., and this division among the elite continued until the end of the republic under the reign of Augustus (r. 27 B.C.E.– 14 C.E.). *See also populares.*

orders The two groups of people in the early Roman republic (founded c. 509 B.C.E.): the patricians who represented wealthy, aristocratic families; and the larger mass of the plebeians, or all the other citizens. Struggle over legal rights and political power caused many conflicts between the Roman orders, resulting in new rights for plebeians to make laws in their own assembly in 287 B.C.E.

Organization of Petroleum Exporting Countries (OPEC) A consortium of oil-producing countries, primarily in Arab nations of the Middle East, founded in 1960 to regulate the supply and exportation of oil. Originally somewhat fragmented, it acted with more unanimity after the United States supported Israel against the Arabs in the wars of the late 1960s and early 1970s, provoking a gas crisis by raising prices in 1973.

orthodoxy A set of beliefs recognized as the correct or true doctrine by religious authorities. The concept of orthodoxy exists among all Judeo-Christian religions. It is most prevalent in

Christianity, which has made concerted efforts to define and enforce orthodoxy either through church councils in the Eastern Orthodox and Protestant sects or under papal authority in the Roman Catholic sect. The early Christian church faced many conflicts that threatened to split the religion; chief among them was the definition of true doctrine and who had the power to name it. Ultimately, bishops from different cities who constituted the church's organization met to stifle disagreement.

Ostpolitik A policy initiated by Willy Brandt, the Socialist mayor of West Berlin, in the late 1960s in which West Germany sought better economic relations with the Communist countries of eastern Europe. It was part of an effort to end or refuse to participate in the cold war and gave West German business leaders the depoliticization of the nation's foreign trade they sought. As a result, trade with eastern Europe expanded rapidly but left poorer countries of the Soviet bloc nonetheless burdened by heavy debt.

ostracism From the Greek *ostrakon* for the broken pottery used as a ballot; Athenian practice of exiling potentially dangerous and influential citizens (c. 460–450 B.C.E.). Once a year, male citizens would vote for the man they thought should be exiled for ten years; the person with the majority of the six thousand ballots cast would be banished, though his property remained his. Ostracism was a method of checking the power of popular individuals who the majority feared might overthrow the democracy and rule as a tyrant.

Ottoman Empire Centered in Turkey, one of the most powerful states in the fifteenth and sixteenth centuries. Although still recognized as a great power, by the middle of the nineteenth century this Muslim region was clearly in decline. The Ottoman Empire formally ended in 1922 with the emergence of the Turkish republic, although the seeds of change began during World War I (1914–1918).

Ottonians The family dynasty that controlled much of Germany following the end of the Carolingian period. The Ottonians get their name from Otto I, who was proclaimed emperor by the pope in 962. Otto and his heirs were politically and militarily strong but faced resistance from local dukes and other powerful nobles who sought to become regional rulers themselves. One of these groups, the Salians, unseated the Ottonians in 1024.

outwork *See* putting-out system.

P

pacifism The belief that war is always wrong and that disagreements and disputes should not be settled by violence. Its advocates embrace peace as the ultimate goal and work through collective action to achieve it. The Sermon on the Mount is often seen as an early call to peace and accounts for a strong pacifist sentiment within Christianity. The Anabaptists of the seventeenth century were early pacifists, as were Quakers and Mennonites. Pacifism was reinvigorated in the 1920s and 1930s thanks to Indian leader Mohandas Gandhi's (1869–1948) doctrine of passive, nonviolent resistance.

palace society The political and social organization of Minoan and Mycenaean civilization (c. 2200–1000 B.C.E.) in which large palace complexes housed both rulers and their political, economic, and religious administrations. The general population clustered their homes around the palaces, with these communities reaching the size of cities. Because they served the dual role of religious leaders and heads of state, Minoan and Mycenaean rulers wielded considerable power.

Paleolithic Literally, "Old Stone"; the first period of the Stone Age, so called because people who lived at that time made their tools from stone. In this era (c. 200,000–10,000 B.C.E.), people did not settle permanently in one place and lived as hunter-gatherers—hunting game, fishing in lakes, and gathering wild grains, fruits, and nuts. *See also* Neolithic.

Pan-Africanism A movement beginning in the early twentieth century that sought both African unity and the removal of colonial powers from the African continent. Formally, it began with the first Pan-African Congress convened in London in 1900. This was followed by several similar congresses attended by intellectuals from both Africa and the Americas. W. E. B. Du Bois (1868–1963), the U.S. writer and political theorist, played a significant mobilizing force in these early congresses. In the 1950s and 1960s, Frantz Fanon (1925–1961), an influential black psychiatrist from Martinique researched and wrote about the trauma affecting colonized people, who daily lived with the threat of violence from the colonizer and the imposition of an outside culture.

Pan-Slavism A movement beginning in the early nineteenth century promoting the cultural and political unity of all Slavs across national and regional boundaries. The first Pan-Slavic conference met in Prague in June 1848 and called for the reorganization of both the Austrian Empire and eastern Europe. It was influenced by the Slavic intelligentsia, who began writing about a common Slavic heritage, and gained momentum after Russia's defeat in the Crimean War (1853–1856). The Pan-Slavic movement ebbed and flowed in succeeding decades, but the achievement of a unified Slavic entity or culture was limited by the differing goals of various groups.

papal monarchy A term used by historians to compare the rule of twelfth-century popes to those of monarchs. Like kings, popes at this time ruled over vast land holdings, had extensive law courts, increasing administrative and financial divisions, and escalating revenue collection. The growing bureaucracy and services provided by the papacy led scholars to regard it as a burgeoning monarchy.

papal states Territories ruled by the papacy. The main papal states were comprised of Rome and most of central Italy, with some states in southern France. The papacy claimed that its Italian states were granted by the Roman emperor Constantine (r. 306–337 C.E.) in the fourth century; however, the so-called Donation of Constantine was determined to be a forgery in 1440. With papal authority undermined during the Great Schism of 1378–1417, the papacy regained control by reaching beyond religious matters into politics, curbing local power, expanding the papal government, increasing taxation, enlarging the papal military, and extending papal diplomacy. The papacy lost its French states during the French Revolution (1789–1799), although it continued to rule its Italian states until Italian unification in 1870.

papyrus Ancient paper first made by the Egyptians and later used by many Western civilizations. Made of processed reeds from the papyrus plant, it was the earliest and most popular form of paper. The arid climate of Egypt allowed for the preservation of many papyrus documents, often found on wrapped mummies or in trash heaps, which provide invaluable information about the ancient world.

Paris Commune Rebel governments that arose to run the city of Paris, first in 1792 after the start of the French Revolution (1789–1799) and, more significantly, in 1871 at the end of the Franco-Prussian War (1870–1871). After the fall of Napoleon III's (r. 1852–1871) government during the latter war, Parisians demanded voting rights, a more balanced distribution of power between the central government and localities, and greater liberties. They declared themselves a self-governing Commune on March 28. Disputes divided the forty-member council, and Napoleon III's provisional government sent in an army to drive the Commune out two months later. Twenty thousand communards died; ten thousand more were deported. Considered a working-class government, the Commune and its demise hold an important place in socialist history. *See also* socialism.

parish   The most basic administrative and territorial organizational unit of the Catholic and mainline Protestant churches, such as Anglican or Episcopal. The parish church provides all of the fundamental religious services for the faithful in its jurisdiction and is overseen at the regional level by bishops or archbishops, who administer a diocese or archdiocese.

parlements   From the French *parler*, "to speak"; high courts in France. Each region had its own parlement, although the most important was in Paris. Parlements could not propose laws, but they could review laws presented by the king and refuse to register them. The king could also insist on their registration. The parlements evolved from the entourages of medieval kings. In the seventeenth century, they became a serious challenge to the expansion of absolutist authority, particularly during the Fronde (1648–1653). *See also* Fronde.

pastoralists   Early nomadic people of the Neolithic era (c. 7000 B.C.E.) who continued to move throughout the Near East in search of grazing land for their sheep, goats, and cattle long after the domestication of farm animals made such movement unnecessary. Pastoralists preferred to travel rather than reside in permanent settlements.

patria potestas   Latin for "father's power"; the legal right of a father in ancient Rome to own the property of his children and slaves and to control their lives. Fathers also held the power of life and death over members of their households, though they rarely exercised it. They did not control their wives, however, since "free" marriages—in which wives formally remained under their fathers' control as long as their fathers lived—became common. A woman without a father was relatively independent, requiring a male guardian to conduct business, but only as a formality. Divorce was simple, with fathers keeping the children.

patrician   A member of the aristocracy in the Roman republic. Until the third century B.C.E., only those descended from noble families could hold political or religious offices. *See also* plebeian.

patron-client system The interlocking network of mutual obligations between Roman patrons (or social superiors) and clients (social inferiors). Originating in the Roman republic (c. 753–44 B.C.E.), the system provided the legal and moral basis for status differences in the society. Patrons helped clients launch political careers by supporting their candidacies and providing loans during hard times. Clients helped patrons' campaigns for office by swinging votes their way or lending money to cover expenses. These relationships were supposed to endure across generations.

Pax Romana The period of relative stability and peace in the Roman Empire in the first and second centuries C.E. The rule of the first Roman emperor, Augustus (r. 27 B.C.E.–14 C.E.), ushered in two hundred years of serenity and prosperity, marred only by brief interludes of fighting between generals striving to rule the empire.

Peace of Augsburg A settlement in 1555 between Holy Roman Emperor Charles V (r. 1519–1556) and the alliance of German Protestant nobles and cities known as the Schmalkaldic League. The agreement ended more than two decades of conflict between the emperor and the league by recognizing the Lutheran church in the empire and allowing princes within the empire to determine whether Catholicism or Lutheranism would be the official religion of their domains. The Peace of Augsburg preserved a fragile peace in central Europe until 1618, but the exclusion of Calvinists planted the seed for future conflict. *See also* Schmalkaldic League.

Peace of God A movement begun by bishops in southern France around 990 C.E. to curb local violence done to property and later (with the Truce of God) to prevent the incessant warfare among local French nobility. By 1050 the movement had become widespread; constituents included bishops, counts, and crowds of lower-class men, and the punishment for violence was excommunication. The Peace of God did stop some local violence but did not address the problem of conflicts between armed men. *See also* Truce of God.

Peace of Paris The series of peace treaties from 1919 to 1920, including the Treaty of Versailles, that provided the settlement and resolution of World War I (1914–1918). These treaties separated Austria from Hungary, reduced the size of Hungary's land by three-quarters, broke up the Ottoman Empire, and treated Germany severely. They destabilized eastern and east-central Europe and ultimately made Germany a pariah. Effectively blamed for the war, Germany was expected to make enormous and economically devastating financial reparations, reduce the size of its army and navy, and cease manufacturing offensive weapons. These measures bred resentment, especially in Germany, Hungary, and states of the Middle East in which England and France took over the governments.

Peace of Utrecht The treaty written between 1713 and 1714 that ended the War of Spanish Succession (1701–1714). The conflict began when Spanish king Charles II (1665–1700) died without an heir and French king Louis XIV (r. 1643–1715) attempted to place his grandson on the throne. Fearing that such an expansion of France's already vast territorial control would upset the balance of power in Europe, major European states formed an alliance to block France's ambitions. The Peace of Utrecht allowed Louis's grandson Philip to ascend the Spanish throne on the condition that he renounce his claim to the French throne, thereby preventing the unification of the two kingdoms. Spain surrendered its territories in Italy and the Netherlands to the Austrians and Gibraltar to the British; France gave up possessions in North America. This treaty marked the end of French dominance in European power politics.

Peace of Westphalia A treaty signed in 1648 that officially ended the Thirty Years' War (1618–1648). The treaty represents a great shift in European power, with the Spanish and Austrian Hapsburgs both losing several territories and France emerging as the main continental power. It was also an important milestone in diplomacy since the terms of the peace were arranged by a congress that met to address international disputes, providing a model for the resolution of future conflicts. *See also* defenestration of Prague.

Peasants' War A massive rural uprising in the central provinces of the Holy Roman Empire in 1525 that signified a crisis in church authority. Inspired by Martin Luther's (1483–1546) anticlerical message and his calls for reforming both church and society, large bands of peasants rose up against their landlords, many of whom were part of the Catholic church hierarchy. The revolt was brutally suppressed, cost more than 100,000 lives, and divided the reform movement. Luther initially tried to mediate the conflict, but later denounced the rebels and advocated the separation of religion and politics. *See also* Protestants.

Peloponnesian League A collection of Greek city-states allied under Spartan leadership with an assembly to decide policy. Following the Persian Wars (499–479 B.C.E.), the rival cities

Athens and Sparta built competing alliances to fortify their positions. The Peloponnesian League was powerful on land, due to Sparta's strong infantry, and at sea, due to Corinth's large navy.

peltlast Light infantry armed with a shield, javelins, and a sword used to supplement the phalanx and increase Athens's military power following its defeat in the Peloponnesian War (431–404 B.C.E.). *See also* phalanx.

penates Roman statuettes depicting spirits of the household stores, including foodstuffs, that were part of Roman household shrines. They were believed to protect the family's health and safeguard the family's moral traditions. *See also* lares.

Pentateuch *See* Torah.

perestroika Russian for "restructuring"; an economic policy instituted in the 1980s by Soviet premier Mikhail Gorbachev calling for the introduction of market mechanisms and the achievement of greater efficiency in manufacturing, agriculture, and services. *See also* glasnost.

Peripatetic School The name given to the Lyceum, the school the philosopher Aristotle founded in Athens in 335 B.C.E. It was named for the covered walkways (peripatos) that students walked under as they conversed on philosophical matters. Along with lecturing on biology, psychology, meteorology, music, and ethics, Aristotle invented a system of logic as the grounds for making a sound case or argument, rather than merely a persuasive one. He also advanced the field and study of ethics.

phalanx The rectangular formation used by Greek hoplites in battle. It relied on soldiers staying in formation and working as a group to achieve military success. *See also* hoplite.

philosophes Eighteenth-century intellectuals of the Enlightenment who wrote on subjects ranging from current affairs to art criticism with the goal of furthering reform in society. While the word means "philosophers" in French, the term is misleading because philosophers wrote about abstract theories, while the philosophes concerned themselves with practical problems of the real world. *See also* Enlightenment.

physiocrats Eighteenth-century economic reformers who sought to apply the Enlightenment principles of individual liberty to agriculture and the economy. Physiocrats promoted a free market and called for the deregulation of the grain trade, the abolition of urban guilds, and a more equitable system of taxation, all of which they believed would encourage productivity. *See also* Enlightenment.

piece rates The payment structure for work in the putting-out system, in which laborers were paid according to the specific part—or piece—of a finished product that they produced rather than by the hour, day, or week. *See also* putting-out system.

pieta Italian for "piety"; a Roman core value representing devotion and duty to family, friends, the state, and the gods. Romans saw core values as divine forces and, as such, linked moral standards and religion. In art, a pieta was a painting or sculpture of the Virgin Mary mourning over Jesus' dead body, commonly used in Renaissance paintings and sculpture.

Pietism A Protestant revivalist movement in the late seventeenth and early eighteenth centuries that, like mysticism, emphasized deeply emotional individual religious experience. Most prominent in the German Lutheran states, Dutch Republic, and Scandinavia, Pietism also had some appeal among Calvinists. *See also* mysticism; Quietism.

Plantagenet Another name for the Angevin dynasty that began its rule of England with Henry II (r. 1154–1189). The word comes from a nickname for Geoffrey V of Anjou (r. 1131–1151), Henry's father, taken from "genet," his favorite shrub. Historians alternate between labeling Henry II's rule as the first Plantagenet or Angevin dynasty. *See also* Angevin.

plantation A large tract of land producing staple crops for the market such as sugar, coffee, and tobacco. Plantations were usually farmed by slave labor and owned by colonial settlers who emigrated from Europe. The plantation system began in Brazil in the early seventeenth century and later spread to the Caribbean and North America.

plebeian The common class of citizens in the Roman republic after 509 B.C.E.; essentially those not included in the aristocracy or patrician class. Plebeians struggled for centuries for the right to hold public office. *See also* patrician.

plebiscites Official resolutions passed by the Plebeian Assembly in Rome. The Plebeian Assembly was created in the fifth century B.C.E. By 287 B.C.E., plebiscites became legally binding for all Romans regardless of social class.

polis An independent city-state based on citizenship that developed in the eighth century B.C.E. Unlike earlier city-states ruled by a monarchy, the Greek polis was a community of citizens, not subjects, who often governed themselves under varying political systems. *See also* city-state.

political state A group of people living in a defined geographic area and organized under a system of government with powerful leaders, officials, and magistrates. Hierarchical, political states first appeared in the Near East following the social changes brought about by the Neolithic Revolution (c. 10,000–8000 B.C.E.) but subsequently emerged throughout the world. *See also* civilization.

politiques Pragmatic political thinkers in late-sixteenth-century France who believed that the development of a durable state took priority over all other political issues, including the question of religion. Influenced by decades of indecisive and destructive religious warfare in France, they believed that religious disputes could be resolved only in the peace provided by a strong government. The politiques carried weight with King Henry IV (r. 1589–1610), who brought an end to the Wars of Religion with the Edict of Nantes in 1598, which granted limited religious freedom to the Protestants.

polyphony Music that consists of two or more melodies performed simultaneously. Before 1215 most polyphony was sacred; the musical form did not become purely secular until the fourteenth century. *See also* motet.

polytheism The worship of multiple gods. The majority of early civilizations, including the Egyptians, Mesopotamians, and Greeks, were polytheistic and worshipped a variety of gods thought to have power over different areas of human existence, such as war, fertility, and weather. *See also* monotheism.

pontifex maximus Latin for "highest priest"; the most important religious official of the Roman world. The pontifex maximus served as the head of state religion and was the ultimate authority on religious matters affecting government. A prestigious political office, many powerful men sought this position, among them Julius Caesar (100–44 B.C.E.), who was elected pontifex maximus in 63 B.C.E.

Poor Law The sixteenth-century English code of law requiring local parishes to care for and provide aid to their impoverished members. These laws underwent significant revision in 1834, when the new Poor Law shifted from an emphasis on outdoor relief, which provided a minimal income but allowed the poor to stay in their homes, to indoor relief, which required the poor to relocate to workhouses. *See also* workhouses.

pop art A style in the visual arts that mimicked advertising and consumerism and that used ordinary objects as part of paintings and other compositions. The movement achieved financial success by the early 1960s. Notable pop artists included American painter Andy Warhol (1928–1987), known for his Campbell's soup–inspired art, and Swedish-born Claes Oldenburg (b. 1929), who portrayed the grotesque aspects of consumer products in his work *Giant Hamburger with Pickle Attached*. Swiss sculptor Jean Tinguely (1925–1991) and partner Niki de Saint-Phalle (1930–2002) used rusted parts of machines to make moveable fountains that adorned squares in Stockholm, Montreal, Paris, and other cities well into the 1980s.

Popular Front An alliance of political parties in places such as France and Spain that united in the 1930s to resist fascism despite deep philosophical differences. *See also* fascism.

populares A Roman political faction comprised of elites who supported the common people. After the death of Gaius Gracchus in 121 B.C.E., the Roman upper class increasingly divided into groups it perceived as supporting its interests and goals. This division continued until the end of the republic under the reign of Augustus (r. c. 27 B.C.E.–14 C.E.). *See also optimates.*

positivism A theory that holds that the diligent study of facts generates accurate, or "positive," laws of society; these laws, in turn, help in the formulation of policy and legislation. Developed in the mid-nineteenth century, positivism is based on the work of the French social philosopher Auguste Comte (1798–1857), and it forms the foundation of the social sciences. Positivism influenced John Stuart Mill (1806–1873) in his bid to extend voting rights to women via a bill in the British House of Commons.

postindustrial A term referring to the moment when the economies of the major world powers shifted from being based predominantly on manufacturing to service industries. The term was used in sociologist David Bell's 1973 book, *The Coming of Postindustrial Society*, in which he argued that Western societies no longer relied on industrial production of goods such as cars or household items for their economic foundations. Instead, service industries such as health care, insurance, education, and financial services had become the largest sector of these economies. The term was also part of a larger linguistic trend to attach the prefix *post* to an array of words, including *postwar* or *postmodern*.

postmodernism A term applied in the late twentieth century to both an intense stylistic mixture in the arts with no central unifying theme or privileged canon and an intellectual critique of Enlightenment and scientific beliefs in rationality and the possibility for precise knowledge. Examples of postmodern art include the AT&T building in New York City; the Guggenheim Museum in Bilbao, Spain; and the "Dancing Building" in Prague, Czechoslovakia, which critics have compared to a crushed soda can.

praetorian guard Soldiers stationed in Rome to protect the emperor and prevent rebellion. Instituted by Augustus (r. 27 B.C.E.– 14 C.E.), the praetorian guard grew in power and sometimes played a critical role in determining imperial succession.

predestination A religious doctrine that holds that God has selected every person for either salvation or damnation before creation. Those who are predestined to be saved, the "elect," are known only to God. Predestination was an important feature in the theology of John Calvin (1509–1564), who took Martin Luther's (1483–1546) doctrine of salvation a step further. Calvin argued that if God is all-powerful and if, as Luther believed, people are incapable of influencing their fate in the afterlife, then God must have determined a person's fate before the beginning of time. *See also* Protestants.

primogeniture The process of inheritance by which the first-born son is the chief beneficiary. Originating after the year 1000, primogeniture maintained a family's possessions, titles, and authority intact in one person's hands. It also left many younger sons without an inheritance or a prospect of marriage; consequently, many lived at the courts of great rulers or joined the church as clerics or monks.

principate The political system created by Augustus (r. 27 B.C.E.– 14 C.E.) in 27 B.C.E. as a disguised monarchy, with the *princeps* ("first man") as emperor. Founded to quell the violence of the previous century, the princeps was originally supposed to be appointed with the approval of the Senate, but in reality, each ruler designated his own heir.

proletarians In the Roman republic (c. sixth century B.C.E.), the masses of people so poor they owned no property or weapons. In government, the proletarian bloc wielded only one vote out of 193; consequently, they were dominated by the elite, wealthier citizens in the assembly.

proletariat The working class or, in Marxist terms, those who do not control the means of production such as factories, tools, workshops, and machines. *See also* communism; Marxism.

propaganda The use of information, usually half-truths, rumors, or even lies, to influence individuals and wider public opinion. Propaganda was widely used by Adolf Hitler (1889–1945) in the 1930s to rally public support for his Nazi Party and its broader agenda. The Nazi Party rose to power by making the seated government look inept and by confronting those who were said to have caused the economic depression Germans faced.

proscription The procedure devised under Roman general Locus Cornelius Sulla of posting a list of those supposedly guilty of treasonable crimes so that they could be executed and their property confiscated. Following his conquest of Rome in 82 B.C.E., Sulla and his henchmen used proscription to eliminate political enemies and increase their personal wealth.

Protestants Members of the Christian branch that formed when Martin Luther (1483–1546) and his followers broke from the Catholic church in 1517. The Protestant movement, known as the Protestant Reformation, also included Calvinists, Anabaptists, and members of the Church of England. The term *Protestant* was first used in 1529 in an imperial diet (parliamentary assembly, traditionally consisting of landholders and other elites) by German princes who protested Holy Roman Emperor Charles V's (r. 1519–1556) edict to repress religious dissent. *See also* Reformation.

Provisional Government The initial government that took control in Russia after the overthrow of the Romanov empire in 1917. The government was composed of aristocrats and members of the middle class, often deputies in the Duma, the assembly created after the Revolution of 1905. The Provisional Government was overthrown by the Bolsheviks led by V. I. Lenin (1870–1924), in 1917. *See also* Bolshevik; Duma.

psychoanalysis Sigmund Freud's (1856–1939) theory of human mental processes and his method for treating their malfunction, primarily through dream analysis. Developed in the late nineteenth and early twentieth centuries, Freud's work challenged existing beliefs that a unified, rational self acted in its own interest. His claims included the then-shocking notions that children have sexual selves and that gender identity evolves from both anatomy and the processing of life experiences. Also known as the talking cure, psychoanalysis had a wide cultural and intellectual impact in the twentieth century, giving rise to a general acceptance of talking about one's problems and a means of recovering mental health.

pump priming An economic policy used by governments to stimulate the economy through public-works programs and other infusions to public funds. The Nazi government relied on this policy in the early to mid-1930s, employing German people to build tanks, airplanes, and a new highway system, thereby reducing unemployment rolls from 6 million to 1.6 million in the four years beginning in 1932.

Punic The Roman word for the people of Carthage, so named because the Carthaginians—wealthy residents of this North African city—were originally from Phoenicia, which in Latin is *Punici*. Carthage controlled an empire encompassing the northwest African coast, part of Libya, Sardinia, Corsica, Malta, and the southern part of Spain. Existing close to the Roman boundary, Carthage seemed both a dangerous rival and a prize to the Romans, who fought three wars with the Carthaginians, from 264 to 241 B.C.E., 218 to 201 B.C.E., and 149 to 146 B.C.E. The third and final Punic War concluded with the destruction of the city of Carthage and Rome's domination of the western Mediterranean.

purges The series of attacks instituted by Russian leader Joseph Stalin (1879–1953) on citizens of the Soviet Union in the 1930s and in later decades as a way of solidifying his power. The victims were accused of being "wreckers" or saboteurs of communism, while the public grew hysterical and pliable because of its fear. Millions across all levels of society were killed or imprisoned as a result, but engineers were the first condemned, charged with low productivity.

Puritans Strict Calvinists who opposed all vestiges of Catholic ritual in the Church of England. The Puritans became influential in the late sixteenth century during the reign of Elizabeth I (r. 1558–1603) and undercut the authority of crown-appointed bishops by placing control of church administration in the hands of a local "presbytery" made up of the minister and the senior members of the congregation. The issue remained a source of tension in the seventeenth century and was a main factor leading to the English Civil War (1642–1646).

putting-out system Also called putting-out work or the "domestic" system; a method of manufacturing widely used for textile production in the preindustrial eighteenth century. Raw materials were distributed to families, who turned them into finished products at home. The putting-out system provided peasant families with supplemental income and allowed manufacturers to escape the restrictions of the urban guilds. The merchant owned the product at every step, but the peasants who typically did the work maintained ownership of the tools of their trade. Although the putting-out system existed for centuries, its flourishing in the eighteenth century expanded beyond textiles to other products such as glassware and guns and helped bring about the Industrial Revolution. *See also* Industrial Revolution.

Q

quadrivium The second, advanced part of the liberal arts education consisting of arithmetic, geometry, musical theory, and astronomy. Introduced in the twelfth century, students interested in quadrivium subjects often studied them apart from the normal curriculum of law, medicine, and theology. Few were able to earn their living through the study of the quadrivium. *See also* trivium.

quantum physics A new kind of physics developed in the early twentieth century that challenged the accuracy of Newtonian physics in terms of subatomic phenomena. Together with Albert Einstein's (1879–1955) theory of relativity, it forms the basis of modern physics.

Quietism A religious revival movement among late-seventeenth-century French Catholics. Popularized by the preaching of Frenchwoman Jeanne Marie Guyon (1648–1717), Quietism shared with the Protestant revival movement Pietism its emphasis on a mystical, emotional, even ecstatic religion. But Quietism emphasized passively absorbing oneself in God's love and, in turn, submitting entirely to divine will. Despite her condemnation of the papacy, Guyon attracted many followers throughout Europe. *See also* Pietism.

quilombo A settlement in the Brazilian backcountry where escaped slaves hid in the seventeenth and eighteenth centuries. The word *quilombo* derived from the Angolan region of Africa, from which many of the Brazilian slaves originated. It also refers to a union of tribes organized for military defense. Quilombos often facilitated the escape of slaves and were routinely targeted by colonial authorities. Some had vast populations in the tens of thousands organized in sophisticated social structures.

quinine A drug made from the bark of the cinchona tree, used to combat the often fatal tropical disease of malaria. The discovery and refinement of quinine in the 1840s made European imperial expansion into formerly impassable areas—especially Africa—possible in the later nineteenth century.

R

racism Any belief, action, or behavior that is based on the idea that human beings are separated into discrete races, with some being superior to others and therefore entitled to dominate or discriminate against the inferior races. Such notions were used to justify slavery and imperialism in earlier periods. Racism continues to be the often unspoken subtext for social, political, and economic prejudices.

radical democracy The ancient Athenian system of democracy, established in the 460s and 450s B.C.E., that extended direct political power and participation in the courts to all male adult citizens. Leaders, however, were still expected to come from the elite classes.

railroads Literally, the tracks on which trains travel; the term later came to refer to the broader system of transportation by train. With their proliferation in the nineteenth century, railroads were emblematic of the power of the Industrial Revolution to transform the environment, the economy, and society in the nineteenth and twentieth centuries by providing faster transportation for people and goods across larger, previously difficult terrain. *See also* Industrial Revolution.

raison d'état French for "reason of state"; a political doctrine in which the interests of the state prevail over all other concerns, most significantly those of religion. The term is most closely associated with Cardinal Richelieu (1585–1642), the French prime minister under Louis XIII (r. 1610–1643). Richelieu, for example, made a political alliance with the Lutheran king of Sweden despite being a leading official of the Catholic church.

The Rape of the Sabine Women A Roman legend about the famous and renowned first king, Romulus. According to the story, Romulus (c. 753 B.C.E.), realizing that the Romans needed more women to bear children and increase the population of the city, begged the neighboring Sabines to let Romans marry their daughters. After being refused, the Romans kidnapped unmarried women at a festival and married them, triggering a war between the Sabines and the Romans. The women begged for peace, and the two peoples merged their populations under Roman rule. The legend illustrates that Rome expanded by absorbing outsiders into its citizenry.

rationalism The philosophy that people must justify their claims by logic and reason, using evidence to back up their conclusions. First developed in Ionia between 650 and 500 B.C.E., rationalism became the foundation for the study of science and philosophy. Due to its rule-based view of the causes of events and physical phenomena, rationalism contrasted sharply with traditional mythology; consequently, many people resisted accepting such a sharp change in their understanding of the world.

realism A style in the arts that depicts society realistically without romantic or idealistic overtones. It arose in the mid-nineteenth century in response to idealistic and heroic art forms, particularly depictions of mythological figures or exaggerated images of noble workingmen. Practitioners included novelist Charles Dickens (1812–1870) and painters Gustave Courbet (1819–1877) and Honoré Daumier (1808–1879).

Realpolitik Policies associated initially with nation building that are said to be based on hard-headed realities rather than the romantic notions or ideals of earlier nationalists. Its goals center on strengthening the state and tightening social order. Originally coined by European leaders following the failed revolutions of 1848, the term has come to mean any policy based on considerations of power alone.

reconquista Spanish for "reconquest"; Christian wars of conquest against the Muslim kingdoms of medieval Spain. Leaders of the reconquista characterized Muslims as outsiders, even though Muslims had been integrated into Spanish society. The Spanish reconquista was connected with the more general crusade movement in Europe and ended in 1492 with the fall of Granada and the expulsion of the remaining Muslims from the kingdom.

redistributive economy An economic system in which officials control the production and redistribution of goods and additionally manage international trade. Based on archaeological evidence, it appears that the early Mesopotamian city-states (c. 3000 B.C.E.) and the Minoans living on Crete (c. 2000 B.C.E.) participated in some form of a redistributive economy.

Reform Act of 1884 The British act that granted the right to vote to a mass male citizenry and doubled the number of voters to 4.5 million. It also enfranchised many urban workers and artisans, thereby reducing the aristocratic influence in the countryside.

Reformation The religious movement founded by Martin Luther (1483–1546), a German friar, in the early sixteenth century, to reform the Roman Catholic church. Outraged by the sale of indulgences and church offices in the local archdiocese of Mainz, in 1517 Luther authored ninety-five theses critiquing the church establishment. Once they became public, they unleashed pent-up resentment and public outrage throughout the Holy Roman Empire. Initially, Luther considered himself the pope's "loyal opposition," offering a series of reforms that he believed would strengthen and improve the church, among them a shift away from the emphasis on good works and toward faith as the key to salvation. Instead, he stressed that Christians could appeal directly to God rather than through good deeds or church authorities. He also assailed corruption within the church, particularly in Italy. Labeled a "protestant" for protesting church theology and practice, his ideas spread rapidly and coincided with similar movements in Switzerland, France, England, and throughout Europe. By the time of Luther's death, half of Europe had left the Roman Catholic church for a variety of new Protestant religions, among them Lutheranism and Calvinism. *See also* Protestants.

Reichstag The lower chamber of the federal parliament of Germany from 1871 to 1945; also, the building that housed the Reichstag and now houses the current German parliament, the Bundestag. Originally established in the fifteenth century to control feuding among the princes and with the emperor, the Reichstag was a national assembly of princes, electors, and representatives from the cities. On its own, it had little power to effect change, but it did convince Emperor Maximilian I (r. 1493–1519) to outlaw private warfare and create a Supreme Court of Justice to keep the peace. When the building caught fire in 1933, Adolf Hitler (1889–1945) used the event to aid in his rise to dictatorial power by blaming communists for setting the blaze. The elections that followed gave a slight majority to Hitler's Nazis, who used their newly achieved power to drive the remaining communists from the Reichstag.

relics The bones, teeth, hair, clothes, and other body parts of a saint, which traditional Christian beliefs hold to be holy because they offer a direct connection to God. They are also believed to produce miracles. Relics are stored in a church dedicated to the given saint. Relics have been monitored and closely scrutinized for authenticity since the Middle Ages; fraud could result in excommunication. Examples of existing relics include pieces of the True Cross and the Precious Blood of Bruges.

reliefs Money payments made on certain occasions by a vassal to a lord as part of the system of obligations. King William I of England (r. 1066–1087), for example, required the payment of reliefs in return for his gifts of land throughout England. *See also* vassalage.

Renaissance French for "rebirth"; a period of revival and flourishing in learning and the arts. The term most commonly refers to the intellectual and artistic movement that began in Italy in the fifteenth century and influenced the rest of Europe in the sixteenth. This Renaissance was characterized by a renewed interest in classical learning and its application to politics, society, and culture. Other important renaissances include the Carolingian renaissance during which Charlemagne (r. 768–814 C.E.) oversaw a revival of arts and learning in his empire in France and Germany, and the twelfth-century renaissance, which witnessed the height of scholasticism, troubadour poetry, and Gothic art.

res publica Latin for "the people's matter" or "the people's business"; the form of government known in modern times as the republic. The Roman republic (c. 509–44 B.C.E.) distributed power widely among male citizens by electing officials in open meetings. It commenced with the exile of the abusive king Tarquin the Proud; because of him, Romans grew to hate and fear the notion of kingship.

restoration The Congress of Vienna's (1814–1815) policy, after the fall of Napoleon I (r. 1804–1814), to "restore" as many regimes as possible to their former rulers, achieve postwar stability by guaranteeing borders, and determine who would hold "great power" status (France, Germany, and Austria, for example) in the new order. This was not always feasible, and in such cases, territories were rearranged to balance the competing interests of the major powers. This system helped prevent another major war until the 1850s, and no conflict comparable to the Napoleonic Wars occurred until 1914.

Risorgimento Italian for "rebirth"; the name given to the movement for Italian unification; it was also a 1850s newspaper edited by Count Camillo di Cavour, prime minister of Piedmont. Efforts to solidify Italy's boundaries existed for centuries but came together under the nationalistic fervor of the mid-nineteenth century. Cavour first sought to retake the provinces of Lombardy and Venetia from the Austrians, and efforts to recombine Parma, Modena, Tuscany, and other areas within a unified Italy ultimately met with success under the military leadership of

Giuseppe Garibaldi (1807–1882). In 1861, the kingdom of Italy was proclaimed.

rococo A style of painting that flourished in the eighteenth century that emphasized irregularity and asymmetry, movement and curvature, but on a smaller, more intimate scale than that of the baroque. By definition, rococo art was meant to be decorative rather than to make a bold religious or political statement. It typically featured scenes of intimate and even erotic sensuality and reflected new sensibilities in art that increasingly attracted a middle-class public. *See also* baroque.

Romanesque The style of art and architecture in western Europe before the twelfth century. Popular in churches, Romanesque architecture emphasized massive stone and masonry walls decorated on the interior with bright paintings. While the form was geometric, sculptural reliefs on the inside and outside were used to enliven the structure.

Romanization The spread of Roman law and culture throughout the provinces of the Roman Empire. Roman influence was greatest in the new cities that sprang up around forts or from settlements of army veterans in western Europe during the Late Republic and Imperial period (c. 44 B.C.E.–284 C.E.). It allowed various peoples throughout the Mediterranean region and mainland Europe access to higher standards of living, increased trade, and more peaceful conditions. Romanization had less effect in the eastern provinces, which largely retained their Greek and Near Eastern characteristics.

romanticism A philosophical and artistic movement of the late eighteenth and early nineteenth centuries that glorified nature, emotion, genius, and the imagination. Romanticism emerged partly in reaction to the Enlightenment's excessive reliance on reason, particularly after the violent excesses of the French Revolution (1789–1799). Closely related to early nationalism, romanticism was also a response to the political turmoil of the Napoleonic Wars and the social upheaval of the Industrial Revolution. *See also* nationalism.

ruler cults Cults that worshipped a ruler as a savior god and existed primarily in the Hellenistic world (c. 323–30 B.C.E.). Members of ruler cults sought protection from fate or bad luck by praying to kings, whose enormous prestige, wealth, and power made them seem godlike. The development of ruler cults proved influential in later Roman imperial religion and Christianity.

Russian Revolution of 1917 Also known as the Bolshevik Revolution, it brought an end to tsarist Russia and ultimately led to the creation of the communist-run Soviet Union. Using Marxist principles, the Bolshevik government that installed itself in 1918 abolished private property, nationalized factories to restore production, and granted universal suffrage to men and women. Its first leader was Vladimir Ilyich Ulyanov, otherwise known as Lenin (1870–1924), followed by Joseph Stalin (r. 1924–1953).

Russification A program starting in the 1860s for the integration of Russia's many nationality groups. Implemented by Tsar Alexander II (r. 1855–1881), it required all residents of Russian territories to adopt the Russian language and the practice of Russian orthodoxy and dispersed ethnic Russians to settle among other nationality groups. It was designed to reduce the threat of future rebellions by national minorities by uniting them culturally.

Russo-Japanese War A conflict between Russia and Japan that took place from 1904 to 1905. It began when Japan, angered by the presence of Russian troops in Manchuria, attacked tsarist forces at Port Arthur. Japan won the war, demonstrating its legitimacy in international relations to the European powers.

S

sacraments Religious rituals performed by Christians that are believed to be essential for salvation. Questions about the validity of the sacraments—how they should be performed and who should be qualified to perform them—represented frequent sources of religious conflict in medieval and early modern Europe. Some, for instance, believed only the most worthy ministers could perform them, but Augustine of Hippo (354–430 c.e.) argued that sacraments were valid regardless of whether the minister's soul was unblemished.

Saint-Simonianism A socialist utopian movement begun in the early nineteenth century by followers of a French noble named Claude Henri de Saint-Simon (1760–1825). In part a reaction to the social upheaval of the Industrial Revolution, Saint-Simonians lived together in cooperative communities where work was shared and less pleasant tasks rotated. Although their advocacy of radical ideas like a "he pope" and "she pope" (ruling father and mother) and free love were scandalous to some members at times, they nonetheless influenced later socialist and liberal ideologies. *See also* Industrial Revolution.

salons Informal gatherings, usually sponsored by middle-class or aristocratic women, that provided a forum for new ideas and an opportunity to establish new intellectual contacts among supporters of the Enlightenment in the eighteenth century. Salons gave intellectual life an anchor outside the royal court and church-dominated universities and afforded an opportunity to test ideas or present unpublished works. Although not exclusive to France, the term is French for "living room," where such gatherings were often held.

samizdat A key form of dissident activity in the Soviet Union and its eastern European satellite countries in the 1960s and 1970s. Individuals reproduced uncensored publications by hand and passed them from reader to reader, thus building a foundation for the successful resistance of the 1980s.

sanitation A concerted effort by governments to protect and improve public health begun in the mid-nineteenth century. Sanitation commissions sought to modernize sewers and remove contaminants from drinking water with the ultimate goal of making cities themselves more healthful. Advocates recognized that eliminating health hazards associated with the water supply and sewage, as well as food handling and urban cleanliness, could reduce disease and epidemics. Cholera, the disease that swept through Asia and Europe in the early 1830s and again from 1847 to 1851, was caused by a waterborne bacteria.

sans-culottes French for "without breeches"; the name given to politically active men from the lower classes during the French Revolution (1789–1799), especially Parisian militants. Sans-culottes wore the long trousers of workingmen rather than the knee breeches of the upper classes. On August 10, 1792, sans-culottes stormed the palace where Louis XVI (r. 1774–1792) and the royal family were staying, setting in motion a chain of events that ended with the downfall of the monarchy.

Saracens Latin for "Arab"; a western European word for Muslims, commonly used in the Middle Ages. It was applied to all Muslims without distinguishing their varying ethnicities, customs, and regional identities; as such it indicated the Western world's lack of knowledge about non-Christian peoples.

Sassanid Empire The dynasty that ruled Persia from 224 C.E. until its conquest by Islamic armies in 651 C.E. The Sassanids were rivals first of the Roman Empire and later the Byzantines. The Zoroastrian kings of the Sassanid Empire controlled a strong military and yet encouraged religious toleration and cultivated writers and scholars. *See also* Zoroastrianism.

satrap A regional, semi-independent governor of the Persian Empire. The office of the satrap was originally an Assyrian government institution, but it was successfully adopted by the Persian king Cyrus (r. c. 557–530 B.C.E.). In the decentralized yet effective Persian system, the satrap's duties included maintaining order, enlisting troops as needed, and sending revenues to the royal treasury.

Schlieffen Plan The German World War I (1914–1919) strategy, named for former chief of the German general staff, Alfred von Schlieffen, that called for attacks on two fronts—concentrating first on France to the west and then turning east to attack Russia. The Germans didn't count on resistance from Belgium in accessing France, which gave the French time to attack the Germans in Alsace and Lorraine and slow the German advance. Germans also faced a long battle and impasse when confronting the British and French armies on the northern front. Such unexpected difficulties kept them from adhering to the light fighting and holding positions of the Schlieffen Plan.

Schmalkaldic League An alliance of German Protestant cities and princes formed in 1531 to resist Holy Roman Emperor Charles V's (r. 1519–1556) efforts to make Catholicism the sole religion of the empire. The league was initially defeated in 1547, but the conflict resumed again in 1552. It continued until Charles V was compelled to sign the Peace of Augsburg in 1555, giving local rulers in the empire the right to determine the religion of their territories. *See also* Peace of Augsburg.

scholasticism The body of theological and philosophical thought of the scholastics, the scholars of medieval universities. Pioneered in the twelfth century by teachers such as Peter Abelard (c. 1079–1144), by the thirteenth century scholasticism's brand of logical inquiry was used to summarize and reconcile all knowledge. Often members of the Dominican and Franciscan orders, the scholastics thought that knowledge obtained through the senses and through reason was compatible with knowledge derived from faith and revelation. St. Thomas Aquinas (c. 1225–1274) was probably the most famous scholastic, and like others, he considered Aristotle (384–322 B.C.E.) the authoritative voice of human reason, which he sought to reconcile with divine revelation in his *Summa Theologiae*. He addressed the keenest concerns of his day, such as whether it was lawful and just to sell something for more than its worth. He concluded that it depended on the circumstances of the buyer and seller, thereby justifying the worldly activities of everyday people.

scientific method A procedure for gathering knowledge through the observation of nature, experimentation, and mathematical deduction. The development of the scientific method in the first half of the seventeenth century challenged previous approaches to knowledge, which emphasized a reliance on the authority of ancient texts, Christian philosophy, and tradition. Among the most important early proponents of the scientific method were Francis Bacon (1561–1626) and René Descartes (1596–1650).

scramble for Africa The late-nineteenth-century process by which European imperial powers carved up the African continent into spheres of influence and areas of direct control. This ultimately led to the complex and messy process of decolonization in the post–World War II period. *See also* spheres of influence.

scutage A monetary payment made by vassals to the English king in lieu of military service. This practice was encouraged by the monarchy of the late twelfth century because vassals were required to serve only for forty days, but hired soldiers—paid with scutage—would fight the king's enemies for as long as they were paid.

Sea Peoples The bands of raiders who devastated much of the eastern Mediterranean in the period of calamities (foreign invasions and wars) between 1200 and 1000 B.C.E. The Sea Peoples were not a single, unified group, but rather a series of assorted invaders of unknown origin who attacked the Egyptians, Hittites, Mesopotamians, and Mycenaeans.

Second International A transnational organization of workers established at a conference in Paris in 1889. Most members were committed to Marxist socialism and sought to address workers' common interests across national boundaries. They advocated labor legislation, suffrage, and a stronger democratic socialist movement. To build support, the Second International determined to rid the group of anarchists and their extreme tactics, instead soliciting the support of workingmen through more affirmative tactics such as songs recognizing their plight and festivals or parades fostering unity. By the early twentieth century, the organization encompassed many of the socialist and social democratic parties of the world.

secularization The process by which a society prioritizes more worldly, political, or social aims over religious practices and beliefs. This shift began in the sixteenth century in western Europe and escalated in the nineteenth century, making religion a matter of private conscience rather than connected to state power and public policy. Secularization did not necessarily involve a loss of faith; rather, nonreligious reasons were used to legitimize political authority and explain natural phenomena. Secularization was most prominent in England, the Dutch Republic, and, to a limited extent, France, and helped set the stage for the scientific revolution.

Seljuk Turks Nomadic Sunni Muslims whose westward migration into areas previously controlled by Byzantium and various local Muslim rulers set off the First Crusade, a holy war in which armed Christians engaged in battles against Muslims in the Holy Land. By 1050 the Seljuk Turks captured the city of Baghdad and subjugated the Abbasid caliphate, the ruling dynasty that drew its power from direct descent from Muhammad (c. 570–632 C.E.) and defeated the Byzantines at the battle of Manzikert in 1071. They then migrated into Asia Minor, eventually controlling much of the peninsula and extending their influence south and east to the city of Jerusalem.

serfdom The system in medieval Europe where peasants were bound to a hereditary plot of land and subjected to the whims of the property owner. England ended the practice before the end of the Middle Ages, in the late eighteenth century Hapsburg followed, and in France it was swept away by the French Revolution (1789–1799). By the nineteenth century, Russia was the only major European power to still hold serfs. The emancipation of the serfs in Russia in 1861 represented one of the most significant achievements of Tsar Alexander II (1855–1881).

serfs Semifree peasants whose status was typically inherited in the Carolingian period (c. 750–900 C.E.) and who were dependent on lords but were not their vassals. Use of serfs developed on a large scale in the Middle Ages in France, Germany, and Spain. Serfs could not legally leave the land they tilled and owed labor services and either produce or money to their lord, whose land it was. They were not slaves and held some rights, including the right to marry, keep part of their produce, and not be unjustly evicted from the land.

signori (singular: *signore*) Lords of Italian cities. As the Italian communes of the thirteenth century became increasingly fractious, regional nobles saw this friction as politically advantageous and offered to become the lords, or signori, of the cities. Their accession to power was often accomplished peacefully, as most communes were willing to accept repression for a lasting peace. *See also* commune.

simony The practice of selling church offices. The term is derived from the name of Simon Magus, a magician in the Christian New Testament who offered St. Peter money to attain the power to confer the Holy Spirit. Simony was a chief target of the Cluniac reform of the eleventh century, which called for a systematic change to improve the church. *See also* Cluniac reform.

Skepticism A philosophy that holds that total certainty about anything is never possible. Originating in ancient Greece, it was revived in the sixteenth century as religious violence and global exploration shook the confidence Westerners had in traditional knowledge. Catholics and Protestants alike balked at the notion since each group was certain that its religion was the right one. By questioning customary authority, skeptical thought opened the way for new ways of thinking about science, religion, and politics.

Slavophilia A form of Russian nationalism in the mid-nineteenth century that opposed efforts to get Russia to follow

Western models of industrial development and constitutional government. Slavophiles instead sought to maintain rural traditions and the centrality of the Russian Orthodox church. They rejected rationality and individualism and sought to protect the country from what they perceived as the corrosion of materialism. The conflict between Westernizers and Slavophiles continues to shape cultural debate in Russia today.

smelting The process of heating ore to remove imperfections from metal. Use of this vital technology may date back to the Neolithic village of Çatalhöyük (c. 6500 B.C.E.) and other sites in the Near East, where traces of slag, smelting's waste remains, were found. This evidence indicates an increase in trade and craft specialization, as well as the growing technological sophistication of Neolithic people.

social contract The doctrine that all political authority derives not from divine right but from an implicit contract between citizens and their rulers. The idea emerged from the writings of Thomas Hobbes (1588–1679) and John Locke (1632–1704) in the second half of the seventeenth century, although each came to different conclusions. Hobbes argued that the social contract gave a ruler absolute power, while Locke claimed it implied a constitutional agreement between a ruler and representatives of their subjects. Rousseau expanded on the theory in 1762, arguing that the contract existed not between a ruler and his or her subjects, but among all members of society, making it every individual's duty to subject their interests to what Rousseau called the "general will."

Social Darwinism A belief that took its inspiration from Darwin's idea of natural selection, arguing that in the economic and political realms, only the fittest would survive. This belief used a distorted version of evolutionary theory to lobby for racist, sexist, and nationalist policies, including the advancement of eugenics. Proponents of Social Darwinism supported a laissez-faire economic strategy and free competition in the business world, arguing that the "unfit" should be allowed to perish in the name of progress. Social Darwinism was used to justify European imperialism and the growing scientific approach to racism in the late nineteenth and early twentieth centuries. *See also* eugenics.

social question An expression common from the 1830s to the 1850s that reflected a widely shared concern about the effects of industrialization and urbanization on the fabric of social life, with particular interest in its impact on the working classes. It pervaded all forms of art and literature, particularly romanticism, which glorified nature and disdained industrialization. Charles Dickens (1812–1870) and other writers similarly sought to show the harsh realities of factory life in literature.

social science   The name given to the nineteenth-century disciplines that sought a scientific study of society, social life, and customs. By the late nineteenth century, anthropology, archaeology, economics, history, psychology, and sociology had all emerged as social sciences.

socialism   A social and political ideology that emerged in the early nineteenth century in response to the upheaval brought about by industrialization. Taking liberalism a step further, socialists advocate a complete reorganization of society and the need to restore social harmony through communities based on cooperation rather than competition. Many nineteenth-century socialists were utopians who believed that the elimination of private property would end social tensions and inspire mutual cooperation. *See also* anarchism; liberalism; Marxism.

Society of Jesus   Also known as the Jesuits; Catholic religious order founded in 1540 by Spanish nobleman Ignatius of Loyola (1491–1556). The Society grew quickly in the sixteenth century and took a leading role in Catholic missionary activity worldwide. The Jesuits were staunch defenders of papal authority and were at the forefront of Catholic reform in Europe. The order also established hundreds of colleges throughout Europe that educated future generations of Catholic leaders.

Socratic method   The type of instruction favored by Socrates (469–399 B.C.E.), the most famous philosopher of Athens's Golden Age. Socrates did not teach through direct instruction, but used a conversational approach in which he asked probing questions to make his listeners examine their most cherished assumptions before arriving at their own conclusions.

Solidarity   An outlawed Polish labor union of the 1980s that contested Communist Party programs and eventually succeeded in ousting the party from the Polish government.

Sophists   From Greek for "men of wisdom"; a new kind of Greek teacher who first appeared around 450 B.C.E. Popular among men with political aspirations such as Pericles (c. 495–429 B.C.E.), Sophists were controversial because they challenged traditional beliefs by teaching new skills of persuasion in speaking and new ways of thinking about philosophy and religion.

The term *sophist* later acquired a negative connotation because they were so clever in debates that they could make deceptive arguments using complex reasoning. *See also* subjectivism.

soviets Councils of workers and soldiers first formed in Russia during the Revolution of 1905. They represented the people in the early days of the 1917 Russian Revolution; because they deposed the tsar (monarch), they saw themselves as a more legitimate political force than the Provisional Government, which saw a battlefield victory as the only way to ensure its position. *See also* Provisional Government.

space age Nickname for the era that began after the successful launch of the Soviet Union's *Sputnik* satellite on October 4, 1957. From that moment on, political leaders turned their focus to the vast possibilities of space, with the major powers seeking to be the first to explore this new frontier. On the cultural front, futuristic television shows, toys, and movies developed, all centered on fantasies about space exploration and its impact on society.

Spanish Armada A naval invasion launched by Philip II of Spain (r. 1556–1598) against England in 1588 with the aim of overthrowing the Protestant Elizabeth I and restoring Catholicism in Great Britain. The Armada was defeated by the English navy, and fewer than half of Spain's ships returned. Spain never fully recovered from the defeat; as such, the Armada represents the beginning of the decline of Spanish power in Europe.

Spanish Civil War A war for control of the Spanish government that enveloped Spain from 1936 to 1939. It was fought between the nationalist right, led by General Francisco Franco (1892–1975), and the Popular Front, a coalition of Socialists, anarchists, Communists, and moderate republicans. The Spanish Civil War became the testing ground for new weapons that were later used in World War II (1939–1945). Heavily financed and supported by Germany and Italy, Franco's efforts prevailed and overthrew Spain's second republican government, with tens of thousands fleeing the country in fear of brutal revenge. *See also* Guernica.

spectacles Shows such as chariot races, mock naval battles, beast hunting, and gladiatorial contests designed to entertain Roman crowds. During the height of the Roman Empire (c. 27 B.C.E.–180 C.E.), spectacles were often organized by the emperor to demonstrate his generosity and power.

spheres of influence Sections of foreign countries in which European imperial powers sought to either establish a colony or an economic and political monopoly, possibly without seeking political control. Spheres of influence were created by treaty, usually between two imperial nations promising not to invade each other's colonies or between the larger country and a representative of the would-be sphere of influence. When first used in the nineteenth century, the term referred to weaker, undeveloped countries that often bordered an existing colony. The definition evolved to include relationships in which one country granted special commercial, legal, and other privileges without direct political involvement. Today it is used to describe regions where more powerful countries claim to have prevailing interests, often to protect their national security.

Sputnik The Soviet satellite successfully launched on October 4, 1957. *Sputnik* caught the U.S. government and public off guard and led to increased funding for U.S. space endeavors. *See also* space age.

stadholder In the Dutch Republic of the mid-seventeenth century, the executive officer chosen by the Estates General to manage the defense of the republic and represent the state in ceremonial occasions. More like a president than a king, the stadholder was usually chosen from the house of Orange.

stagflation The unusual combination of a stagnant economy and soaring inflation that emerged in Europe, the Soviet Union, and the United States in the 1970s as a result of an OPEC embargo on oil. *See also* Organization of Petroleum Exporting Countries (OPEC).

Stoicism The Greek philosophy that taught that although individuals are controlled by fate, they should still make the pursuit of virtue their goal. A Stoic person could put himself in harmony with nature by cultivating good sense, justice, courage, and temperance. Founded by Zeno (c. 333–262 B.C.E.), Stoicism was named for the Painted Stoa in Athens, where Stoic philosophers discussed their doctrines.

stream of consciousness A style of writing that eschews traditional narrative and argument in an attempt to give the reader access to the thoughts and feelings of a character. It was first used by Édouard Dujardin (1861–1949) in 1888 and made famous in the English-speaking world by writers such as James Joyce (1882–1941) and Virginia Woolf (1882–1941). The style emerged in reaction to World War I (1914–1918), the rise of

Sigmund Freud's (1856–1939) psychoanalysis, women's ongoing struggle for equality, and other social changes in the early twentieth century. Writers like Woolf felt that the solid society with its intriguing characters had dissolved, replaced instead by fragmented conversations and incomplete and interrupted relationships. *See also* psychoanalysis.

subjectivism The philosophy that stresses that there is no absolute reality behind and independent of appearances. The Greek Sophist Protagoras (c. 485–410 B.C.E.), who taught in Athens after 450 B.C.E., espoused a form of subjectivism that emphasized two main ideas: first, that human institutions and values are only matters of custom, convention, and law and not creations of nature; and second, that since truth is subjective, speakers should be able to argue both sides of a question. *See also* Sophists.

Successor Kings Generals of Alexander the Great (r. 336–323 B.C.E.) who carved out their own kingdoms following his death in 323 B.C.E. Antigonus (c. 381–301 B.C.E.) took Anatolia, the Near East, Macedonia, and Greece; Seleucus (c. 358–281 B.C.E.) seized Babylon and the East; and Ptolemy (c. 367–282 B.C.E.) obtained Egypt. The Successor Kings had to rely on military might, prestige, and ambition to successfully rule their new territories.

Suez Canal A one-hundred mile canal in Egypt connecting the Red Sea and Indian Ocean with the Mediterranean Sea. Designed by the French, the canal was completed in 1869 with investments from Great Britain and France and quickly became both economically and strategically important by shortening the route from Europe to Asia. Great Britain began to gain control of the canal in 1875 and formally took control during its occupation of Egypt in 1879. By 1888, the Treaty of Constantinople made the canal a neutral zone. But not until Egypt gained its independence from Britain in 1952 did it reclaim the canal. When Egyptian president Gamal Abdel Nasser (1918–1970) nationalized the Suez Canal in 1956, he became a hero to Arabs in the region.

suffragists A movement beginning in the middle of the nineteenth century that sought to extend voting rights to women. The suffrage movement became an increasing political force in the early twentieth century, though not until after World War I (1914–1918) did many Western nations begin to grant women the right to vote.

summa (plural: summae) Developed in the twelfth century, a systematic, authoritative, and exhaustive exploration of a topic offering every possible meaning and resolution. Based on the philosophy of Aristotle (384–322 B.C.E.), topics ranged from human morality, the physical world, society, belief, action, and theology. The summa was considered a first step in spreading knowledge: once it was written, the scholar was expected to share his conclusions by presenting them to the public. Summae were also meant to be the last word on a given subject. One of the more famous summae was *Summa Theologica* by Thomas Aquinas (1225–1274), in which he offers five arguments proving God's existence.

Sunday school movement A movement that pushed religious education for children, particularly working-class children, in nineteenth-century Great Britain. Founded by Robert Raikes (1735–1811), the idea became widespread by the 1840s and 1850s, especially in Protestant countries. Sunday schools often taught children how to read and write at a time when working children were unable to go to school during the week. As such, it was an important part of the movement toward universal education.

superpower A term designating a nation-state that holds a leading position in world politics and economics. It was used after World War II (1939–1945) as a label for the only two powerful countries remaining—the United States and the Soviet Union—and use of this label solidified during the cold war. Currently, the United States is acknowledged as the world's only superpower.

sweatshop A term of derision for a factory with low wages, long hours, and harsh or unsafe working conditions. The term comes from the British slang *sweat*, an owner who employed workers for mind-numbing tasks at poor wages. Sweatshops emerged in Great Britain in the early nineteenth century but were outlawed by the early twentieth. Nonetheless, by the early twentieth century, the term became synonymous with garment and textile factories. Sweatshops remain prevalent today in the developing world, often producing goods cheaply for more advanced countries.

Swiss Confederation An alliance of towns and peasant communes in the Swiss Alps that later became the modern state of Switzerland. Formed in 1291, the confederation defeated a Habsburg army in 1315 to rid themselves of their oppressive overlord and establish a new and free alliance. Part of a more general trend of fragmentation of the Holy Roman Empire in the fourteenth century, the Swiss Confederation represented the growth of self-governing peasant communities in the Alpine Valley.

symposium (plural: symposia) A social for Greek men that involved much drinking and entertainment, including music, poetry, philosophical discussion, and hired female companions known as hetaira.

Synod of Whitby A meeting of churchmen in England in 664 C.E. to determine the type of Christianity the English people would follow. It was organized by Oswy, the king of Northumbria (r. 655–670 C.E.), to resolve the conflicts and discrepancies between Irish and Roman Christianity, in particular the correct date of Easter. Oswy believed that Roman Christianity was the true voice of the church, and his position paved the way for the triumph of the Roman church in England.

syphilis A highly contagious, sexually transmitted disease that has plagued societies since at least the fifteenth century. It was untreatable until the development of Salvarsan by Nobel Prize–winning German scientist Paul Ehrlich (1854–1915) in 1909. Historians debate its origins, some claiming it began in the New World and was transferred back to Europe by explorers, in particular Christopher Columbus's crew; others say it dates back to ancient civilization but was not recognized apart from other diseases like leprosy. In more advanced untreated cases, this bacterial infection can damage the heart, brain, nervous system, and eyes—even leading to mental illness or death. King Henry VIII of England (r. 1509–1547) and German philosopher Friedrich Nietzsche (1844–1900) allegedly died from complications of the disease.

T

Table of Ranks A codification of legal and social relationships in Russia, written in 1722 by Tsar Peter the Great (r. 1682–1725). Enduring for two centuries, it made social status—and all social and material advantages—dependent on service to the state (military, administrative, and court) and gave the tsar unprecedented control over the Russian nobility.

tagmata Mobile Byzantine armies created after 850 C.E. to support the aggressive expansion of the Byzantine borders. Composed of the best troops, the tagmata helped add more territory to the Byzantine Empire than it had possessed in several hundred years. It had previously lost much territory, including the Balkans, after a series of wars and conquests.

taifas The small, independent kingdoms of Islamic Spain after the collapse of the caliphate of Cordoba in 1031. A lack of cooperation and disunity among the taifas ultimately aided the Christian conquest of Spain.

temperance A nineteenth-century movement across Europe and the United States that called for abstinence from alcohol as a way of supporting a moral, upstanding lifestyle. It was supported by both Catholics and Protestants, who saw drunkenness as a sign of moral weakness and a threat to the social order, particularly to families. Industrialists, too, embraced temperance because they linked low worker productivity and lack of discipline to overuse of alcohol. The temperance movement eventually led to the prohibition of alcohol in the United States from 1919 to 1933 and Finland from 1919 to 1931.

Tennis Court Oath A pledge taken by reform-minded deputies of the Estates General on June 20, 1789, to create a constitution for France. On that day, the Third Estate, representing the more than 95 percent of French people who were not part of the clergy or nobility, were locked out of their usual meeting hall following a dispute with Louis XVI (r. 1774–1792). The disagreement centered on whether voting in the Estates General should be done by estate—which would have given the nobility and the clergy a majority—or by the number of delegates. Members of the Third Estate met in a nearby tennis court with sympathetic nobles and clergymen, swearing not to disband until they produced a constitution. This event represented a turning point in the French Revolution (1789–1799).

Terror A radical phase in the French Revolution (1789–1799) led by Maximilien Robespierre (1758–1794), which sought to create a "republic of virtue" in which the government would teach—or force—citizens to become virtuous republicans through a massive program of reeducation. In 1793 the Committee of Public Safety was established to direct this effort, using the guillotine to suppress dissent; tens of thousands of ordinary citizens were executed. The Terror ended in July 1794 when the National Convention rose up against Robespierre and sent him to the guillotine. *See also* Committee of Public Safety; Thermidorian Reaction.

terrorism Coordinated and targeted political violence by opposition groups, often designed to have both military and psychological consequences on its victims. The term derives from the eighteenth-century French Revolution's Reign of Terror (1793–1794). In the twentieth century, terrorism was used by the Irish Republican Army and the Palestinian Liberation Organization as part of a broader strategy for self-rule. Throughout the 1980s, terrorists from the Middle East and North Africa planted bombs in many European cities, blew up airplanes, and bombed the Paris subway system. The attacks on September 11, 2001, were seen as unleashing a modern terrorist era, first in the United States with the attacks on the World Trade Center and the Pentagon and later globally in countries like Spain and Britain where train and rail systems were bombed.

tertiaries Laypepole who affiliated themselves with the friars after the twelfth century. Attracted to the increasing popularity of the mendicants (monks who earned their living from begging or alms), they adopted many of their pious practices, such as charity and prayer, while still living in the world, raising families, and fulfilling their occupations.

Tetrarchy Literally, "rule of four"; the system of government instituted by Diocletian (r. 284–305 C.E.) to run the Roman Empire after his victory in 293 C.E. Diocletian divided the empire into four administrative districts, two in the east and two in the west. He ruled one district and appointed three junior partners to govern the others. It effectively ended Rome's thousand years as the capital city, replacing it with four new capitals. Although Diocletian's successors discontinued the formal Tetrarchy after his abdication in 305 C.E., its principle of subdivision endured in Roman imperial rule.

Thatcherism Political and economic policies associated with British prime minister Margaret Thatcher in the 1980s, which were based on supply-side economics. Using these policies to stimulate the economy, the British government cut income taxes on the wealthy to spur new investment and increased sales taxes to compensate for the lost revenue, the latter of which was difficult for working people. Thatcher also scaled back government intervention in the economy, selling publicly owned businesses and utilities such as British Airways, refusing aid to outmoded industries such as coal mining, and slashing education and health programs. These moves were designed to stimulate growth from the top, eventually trickling down to the rest of society.

thaw The climate of relative toleration for free expression in the Soviet bloc after the death of communist leader Joseph Stalin (1879–1953). The thaw alternated with periods when the government returned to repression.

themes The military districts that composed the Byzantine Empire beginning in the seventh century C.E. Each was commanded by a general or "strategos." To safeguard against frontier attacks, generals lured landless men to join the army in exchange for land and low taxes. This successful strategy ultimately shifted the focus to rural life with long-term consequences for Byzantine education and culture.

Thermidorian Reaction The violent backlash in France against the rule of Maximilien Robespierre (1758–1794) that began with his arrest and execution in July 1794, or 9 Thermidor in the French revolutionary calendar. Most of the instruments of the Terror were dismantled, Jacobins were purged from public office, and Jacobin supporters were harassed or even murdered. *See also* Jacobin Club; Terror.

Third Republic The government that succeeded Napoleon III's (r. 1852–1871) Second Empire after its defeat in the Franco-Prussian War of 1870–1871. It adopted a new constitution building on existing liberties and creating a ceremonial presidency and a premiership dependent on support from an elected Chamber of Deputies. To rally citizens, leaders fortified civic institutions including compulsory and free public education in the 1880s and mandatory military service for young men. Despite corruption from within, the Third Republic lasted until France's 1940 defeat in World War II (1939–1945).

third world A term devised after World War II (1939–1945) to designate those countries outside either the capitalist world of the U.S. bloc or the socialist world of the Soviet bloc—most of them emerging from imperial domination. It also indicated countries that were less industrialized than the Western or Soviet regions.

Thirty Tyrants Spartan oligarchy established to rule Athens following the city's defeat in the Peloponnesian War (404 B.C.E.). This pro-Spartan, antidemocratic, and repressive regime ruled for only eight months; it was ultimately ousted by prodemocratic forces.

tithe A tax equivalent to a portion, typically one-tenth, of a parishioner's annual income or crops taken by the church. Long a tradition in Judaism, tithing was first instituted by the Roman Catholic church in the eighth and ninth centuries C.E.

Torah The first five books of the Hebrew Bible, also known as the Pentateuch. The Torah, written about 950 B.C.E., provides many of the laws and traditions for the Jewish people to follow, including the Ten Commandments.

Tory One of two political factions that developed in the English Parliament in the late seventeenth century over the succession of the Catholic king James II (r. 1685–1688) to the throne. Unlike their Whig adversaries, Tories supported James II despite his Catholicism and advocated a strong hereditary monarchy. They also embraced the ceremonial aspects of the Anglican church, to which many Protestants had been opposed. In the mid-nineteenth century, the Tories evolved into the Conservative Party. *See also* Whig.

total war A war built on full mobilization of soldiers, civilians, and the technological capacities of the nations involved. Often highly destructive, total war also involves a struggle over prevailing ideas and ideologies. With over forty million wounded or killed in battle, World War I (1914–1918) is typically characterized by historians as a total war.

totalitarianism A single party form of government emerging after World War I (1914–1918), in which the ruling political party saturates all parts of the social, cultural, economic, and political life of the population. A totalitarian state typically makes effective use of mass communication and violence to instill its ideology and maintain power. Though no state has been completely totalitarian, the term is particularly associated with Nazi Germany, Fascist Italy, and Stalinist Russia.

travel literature A genre of popular literature in seventeenth- and eighteenth-century Europe in which writers shared accounts of their travels and contrasted their homelands with other cultures. As trade and colonization increased, tales of European contact with other civilizations began to circulate widely among the reading public. Travel literature led many Europeans to question the superiority of Western values and society because these stories often portrayed people who were better off without the supposed advantages of Western civilization.

The Travels of Marco Polo Published in the second half of the thirteenth century, the account of Italian merchant Marco Polo's (1254–1324) voyage to China. Although it contains many inaccuracies, especially about the distances involved in his trip, it helped inspire future explorers, such as Christopher Columbus (1451–1506). It was a leading source of information on the East during its time and continued to influence Western conceptions of East Asia for many centuries thereafter.

Treaty of Brest-Litovsk Peace agreement signed by Russia and the Central Powers—Germany, Austria-Hungary, Bulgaria, and the Ottoman Empire—on March 3, 1918, which ended hostilities between the two sides during World War I (1914–1918). The treaty's terms spelled significant losses for Russia by placing vast areas of the old Russian Empire under German occupation and partially realized Germany's ideal of a central European region. With millions of square miles gone, the Bolsheviks used this opportunity to consolidate their power: they moved the capital from Petrograd to Moscow and formally adopted the name Communist. Bolshevik leader V. I. Lenin (1870–1924) agreed to the treaty's harsh terms in part to deliver on the peace he promised, but also because he believed that the rest of Europe would soon rebel and overthrow capitalism.

Treaty of Lodi A peace agreement signed in 1454 that ended decades of war between the major Italian city-states brought on by Milanese expansionism. The high mark of Renaissance diplomacy, the treaty established a complex balance of power on the Italian peninsula and maintained stability until France invaded in 1494.

Treaty of Verdun The treaty signed by the heirs of Louis the Pious (r. 814–840 C.E.) following his death in 840. After a decade of fighting for political primacy, Louis's heirs agreed in 843 to restore the peace by dividing the empire into three distinct kingdoms run by each of the brothers. The treaty marked the end of Charlemagne's (r. 768–814) European-wide empire and defined the future political contours of western Europe. The western third bequeathed to Charles the Bald (r. 843–877) became France; the eastern third handed to Louis the German (r. 843–876) became Germany; the Middle Kingdom given to Lothair (r. 840–855) was eventually absorbed partly into France and Germany, with the rest forming the Netherlands, Belgium, Luxembourg, Switzerland, and Italy.

Treaty of Versailles The central component of the Peace of Paris (1919–1920), which effectively ended World War I (1914–1918). The Treaty of Versailles returned Alsace and Lorraine to France, led to temporary occupation by France of parts of Germany, limited Germany's military, and levied substantial monetary reparations on the German government, effectively blaming Germany alone for the war. Ultimately, the treaty's harsh burdens led to the destabilization of Germany and indirectly contributed to the rise of the Nazi Party. *See also* Peace of Paris.

trench warfare A combat style in which soldiers dug deep trenches along either side of a contested area, often along the front line. Although it was used in the U.S. Civil War (1861–1865), trench warfare became widely prevalent during World War I (1914–1918), especially on the western front, in response to the new offensive firepower of machine guns and mustard gas. With the emergence of the tank as an offensive weapon, trench warfare was far less common in World War II (1939–1945).

triangle trade *See* Atlantic system.

tribune A political office created circa 450 B.C.E. to provide plebeians a voice in Roman government. Tribunes were a special panel of ten annually elected officials whose only duty was to stop actions that would harm plebeians or their property. The establishment of this office paved the way for plebeians to ultimately serve in all ranks of the government.

tribute An obligatory tax or payment made by a feudal vassal (one who pledges services and allegiance) to a lord, his better, in the Middle Ages. Tributes were also made by rulers or nations to acknowledge their submission to another ruler or to cover the cost of protection, and they could be in the form of money, gifts, or other commodities.

Triple Alliance A treaty between Austria, Germany, and Italy signed in 1882 that called for joint response if any one of the signatories were attacked. It was fundamental to the diplomatic structure of World War I (1914–1918).

trireme An ancient Greek warship outfitted with a ram, equipped with sails, and rowed by 170 oarsmen sitting on three levels. The trireme was the main ship of the powerful Athenian fleet during the Peloponnesian War (431–404 B.C.E.), and its size and expense meant it could be built only by the wealthiest city-states.

trivium The first three—the foundational subjects—of a liberal arts education: grammar, rhetoric, and logic. *See also* quadrivium.

troubadours Lyric poets who first appeared in the twelfth century in southern France and sang of love, longing, and courtesy. Their poetry, which was played at many royal courts, emphasized the power of women and was immensely popular throughout France, Italy, England, and Germany.

Truce of God A second movement in southern France to curb military violence. It supplemented the existing Peace of God movement (c. 1050 C.E.) by forbidding fighting on specific days of the week (Thursday through Sunday). This prohibition was enforced by local knights and nobles, who swore oaths over saints' relics to uphold it. *See also* Peace of God.

tsar (czar) The Russian imperial title first taken by Muscovite prince Ivan III (r. 1462–1505). The last Russian tsar, Nicholas II (r. 1894–1917), held fast to orthodoxy in religion, autocracy in politics, and anti-Semitism and Russification in social policy. Forced to abdicate in 1917 as a result of the Russian Revolution, he and his family were later executed by a group of Bolsheviks, members of the party that had seized power. *See also* Bolshevik.

tuberculosis A highly infectious respiratory disease that reached epidemic levels in the eighteenth and nineteenth centuries in areas of rapid industrialization and urbanization. Tuberculosis was the leading cause of death in the West until the twentieth century. Although it declined due to improvements in health care and hygiene, it has never been completely eradicated.

Twelve Tables The first written Roman code of law, named after the bronze tablets on which it was engraved. Enacted between 451 and 449 B.C.E., the Twelve Tables prevented magistrates from arbitrarily abusing their power and thus became an important symbol of justice to the Roman people.

U

U-boat Abbreviated from *unterseeboot*; a German submarine. Although primitive submarines were developed as early as the U.S. Civil War (1861–1865), it was not until World War I (1914–1918) that they became viable as weapons. In May 1915, German submarines sank the British passenger ship *Lusitania*, killing 1,198 people, including 124 Americans. Outraged, the United States initially maintained its position of neutrality, but the use of unrestricted submarine warfare in World War I by Germany brought the United States into the war by April 1917.

Umayyad caliphate The ruling dynasty of the Islamic world and direct successors of Muhammad (c. 570–632 C.E.). Under the Umayyad caliphs from 661 to 750 C.E., the Muslim world became a state. This first caliphate was a period of settlement, new urbanism, and literary and artistic flourishing. Arabic was the standard language of the Umayyad government and throughout its territory. *See also* caliphs.

ummah Arabic for a community of believers sharing a belief in one God and a set of religious practices. Muhammad's (c. 570–632 C.E.) emphasis on loyalty to the whole of the ummah over the individualism of the tribe allowed Islam to serve as a binding force for the converted.

Unionization The process by which workers at a particular location or industry come together to form a negotiating bloc to seek better wages and working conditions. Union movements began in the early phases of the Industrial Revolution, first in Britain, then in the rest of Europe and North America. Unions were central in gaining better wages and working conditions for their members throughout the nineteenth and twentieth centuries. They also exercised considerable political power and continue to do so. *See also* Industrial Revolution.

United Nations (UN) An organization for collective security and deliberation set up as World War II (1939–1945) closed. Beyond international peace, its mission includes developing friendly relations between countries and solving conflicts through cooperation. Headquartered in New York City, it replaced the ineffective League of Nations and has proved active in resolving international conflicts both through negotiation and the use of force. Beginning with the United States and the Soviet Union as members, the UN grew to represent over 190 member nations. It has aided in conflicts such as the Arab-Israeli wars of 1967 and 1973 and the 1963 Cuban missile crisis. The UN Security Council is charged with peacekeeping efforts and can take any measures deemed necessary to secure peace, playing a role in the Persian Gulf War and overseeing Cambodian elections in 1993.

universities From Latin for "guild"; medieval centers of scholarship and learning restricted to men and providing valuable services to kings and popes. Universities originally developed in the thirteenth century as guilds of students and masters in places such as Paris, Bologna, and Oxford. The word eventually came to mean an institution of higher learning itself. Early universities often maintained distinct specialties: Bologna was principally a school of law, while Paris emphasized the liberal arts and theology. Some also maintained close ecclesiastical ties, but during the nineteenth century, universities were reorganized and secularized. In the modern era, universities became the site of critical scientific, technological, and sociological research. Some began admitting women in the late nineteenth and early twentieth centuries. *See also* guilds.

urbanization The process by which formerly rural areas and small towns and cities grew in size and population. Beginning in the nineteenth century and fueled by industrialization, city populations in Western nations dramatically increased— nearly doubling in some countries—by midcentury, as people sought factory and other jobs in new urban centers. The rapid growth in the early phases of urbanization led to overcrowding, poor sanitation, and disease, however, for many of the inhabitants.

utilitarianism A liberal ideology promoted by English philosopher Jeremy Bentham (1748–1832). Based on the writings of John Locke (1632–1704), it argues that the best social and political policies are those that produce—in Bentham's words—"the greatest good for the greatest number" and are therefore the most useful, which, to him, meant liberalism. Liberals supported the Enlightenment ideas of increased personal liberty and free trade in economics. *See also* Enlightenment; liberalism.

V

vassalage A system of obligations, rights, and duties a free person or institution owed to the individual or entity on which he was dependent. Vassalage developed in the ninth century in response to a lack of central authority; as power increasingly fell into the hands of local lords, these lords required faithful men, or vassals, to defend them. Poor vassals, on the other hand, looked to their lords for financial aid. The system often involved a free warrior who was nonetheless dependent on a lord, but it was not limited to warriors. Monasteries often had knights as vassals, and abbots were often the vassals of powerful lords.

Vatican II A Catholic council held between 1962 and 1965 to modernize some aspects of church teachings (such as condemnation of Jews), to update the liturgy, and to promote cooperation among the faiths (i.e., ecumenism). It was initiated by Pope John XXIII (r. 1958–1963) in response to a perceived crisis in faith caused by increased affluence and secularism. In the last session in 1965, the council renounced the longstanding church doctrine that condemned the Jews for killing Christ. John's successor, Paul VI (r. 1963–1978), however, maintained the church's position against the use of artificial birth control.

vernacular literature Works written in the languages spoken by the people as opposed to being written in Latin. Vernacular literature began to flourish in the fourteenth century and is exemplified by the works of Francesco Petrarch (1304–1374), Giovanni Boccaccio (1313–1375), and Geoffrey Chaucer (c. 1342–1400). Unlike medieval troubadours, whose work was typically written for and by people with aristocratic backgrounds, vernacular literature was written by people of urban, middle-class origins for a literate laity. Its emergence represented an aesthetic shift away from Latin and the church, previously the dominant force in Europe's intellectual life.

Vestal Virgins The only Roman priesthood for women in the Roman republic (509–27 B.C.E.). The Vestal Virgins were six unmarried women sworn to chastity at the ages of six and ten for thirty years who tended the shrine and eternal fire of Vesta, the Roman goddess of the hearth and protector of the family. This granted them high status in Roman society and freed them from their fathers' control. On rare occasions when the flame died out, Romans assumed one of the Virgins had broken her vow of chastity and buried her alive as punishment.

Victorian era Generally, a term referring to most of the nineteenth century in western Europe and North America, as defined by the reign of Queen Victoria of Great Britain (r. 1837–1901). The term *Victorian* came to denote social and cultural conservatism marked by concern for good manners, modesty, propriety, and often prudery.

Viet Minh The Vietnamese independence movement founded by the European-educated Ho Chi Minh (1890–1969) in 1941 to fight colonial rule. He advocated the redistribution of land held by big landowners, especially in the rich agricultural area in southern Indochina. Guerrilla fighters ultimately forced the technologically superior French army to withdraw in 1954. The Viet Minh was eventually absorbed into the Lao Dong, the Vietnamese Workers' Party, although elements also joined the Viet Cong.

Vikings A Scandinavian people who raided and eventually expanded into parts of Russia, England, and France. Both merchants and pirates, the Vikings began their independent raids at the end of the eighth century. Over time, many settled in diverse parts of Europe, establishing kingdoms in Normandy, England, and Kievan Russia. *See also* Kievan Russia.

Visigothic Spain A term referring to Spain under the rule of the Visigoths from the fifth century until the Islamic conquest in 711. The Visigothic kingdom originally stretched across much of southern France and northern Spain; however, following a defeat by the Franks in 507, the Visigothic kingdom was confined to the Iberian peninsula. Visigothic rulers were originally Arian but converted to Catholicism under King Reccared (r. 586–601) in 587. This conversion led to a level of cooperation between church and state that was unprecedented in other regions. *See also* Arianism.

Vulgate The Latin version of the Bible and the only version authorized by the Roman Catholic church until modern times. According to tradition, the Vulgate Bible was translated from Hebrew, Greek, and Aramaic by St. Jerome in the late fourth and early fifth centuries. The word *vulgate* means "common" or "popular" and refers to the fact that this version was written in a common type of Latin rather than a more formal, literary version. It contained many translation errors, which were challenged by humanists during the Renaissance. Because few people in the Middle Ages understood Latin, the Vulgate Bible gave the clergy a virtual monopoly on the Scriptures, which was subsequently challenged during the Protestant Reformation by Martin Luther and others with their own vernacular translations.

W

war guilt clause The part of the Treaty of Versailles that assigned blame for World War I (1914–1918) to Germany. The clause was the source of much resentment in Germany, a fact the Nazi Party was able to use in bolstering its rise to power in the 1930s. *See also* Peace of Paris; Treaty of Versailles.

Wars of the Roses An intermittent series of civil wars that occurred in England between 1455 and 1485 fueled by factional rivalry among the nobility—the House of York and the House of Lancaster—as well as regional discontent. The war was so named because of the houses' symbols—a white rose for York, a red rose for Lancaster. The wars began when Richard of York rebelled against the mentally unstable king Henry VI (r. 1422–1461) and ended when Henry Tudor was crowned Henry VII (r. 1485–1509). Despite the length of the conflict, it caused little disruption in England, whose economy continued to expand.

Warsaw Pact A military alliance between the Soviet Union and its satellite communist nations set up in 1955 as a counter to the North Atlantic Treaty Organization (NATO). Its members included Bulgaria, Czechoslovakia, East Germany, Hungary, Poland, Romania, and the Soviet Union. It ceased to exist in 1991 after the collapse of communism in the Soviet Union and eastern Europe. *See also* North Atlantic Treaty Organization (NATO).

Weimar Republic The parliamentary republic established in 1919 in Germany to replace its previous imperial form of government and named for the city where it first met. Culturally vibrant, the republic helped Germany become a center for experimentation in the arts, even while it remained on politically unstable ground. As economic depression continued to plague the country, the Weimar Republic became increasingly politically ineffective until its demise at the hands of Adolf Hitler (1889–1945) and the Nazi Party.

welfare state A system comprising state-sponsored programs for citizens, including veterans' pensions, social security, health care, family allowances, and disability insurance. Most highly developed after World War II (1939–1945), the welfare state existed on both sides of the cold war; it intervened in society to bring economic equality by setting a minimum standard of well-being.

wergild Money or goods a murderer had to pay in compensation for his crime. Under Frankish law as codified by King Clovis (r. 481–511 C.E.) between 507 and 511 C.E., the majority of the wergild went to the victim's relatives, with about one-third paid to the king. Wergild demonstrates the importance of rank in Frankish society; murderers paid vastly different amounts based on their victims' social status.

Westernization The effort, especially in Peter the Great's (r. 1682–1725) Russia, to make society and social customs resemble its counterparts in western Europe, especially France, Britain, and the Dutch Republic. The program of Westernization included adopting Western dress, replacing the traditional Russian calendar with a Western one, introducing public newspapers, recruiting foreigners to serve as consultants and advisors, expanding and modernizing the army, and moving the capital from Moscow to St. Petersburg, which was built according to Western design. In the Middle East, Mustafa Kemel (1881–1938) led the Turks to establish an independent republic and capitalist economy in 1923. He changed the capital city's name from Constantinople to the Turkish Istanbul in 1930, mandated Western dress for men and women, introduced the Latin alphabet, and abolished polygamy. Efforts at Westernization met resistance among traditionalists.

Whig One of two political factions that developed in the English Parliament in the late seventeenth century over the succession of the Catholic king James II (r. 1685–1688). Unlike their Tory counterparts, Whigs opposed the ascension of James to the throne, favored parliamentary supremacy, and advocated toleration for Protestant dissenters against the Anglican church. In the mid-nineteenth century, the Whigs evolved into the Liberal Party. *See also* Tory.

white-collar An adjective describing service sector office workers and professionals, as opposed to manual laborers or those employed in industry or manufacturing, who are known as blue-collar workers. The term first appeared with the rise of the modern office in the final decades of the nineteenth century and described the new categories of so-called clean jobs—secretary, file clerk, or typist—available to educated, middle-class men initially and women later.

wisdom literature Fables, essays, proverbs, and prophecies in both prose and poetry that taught morality and proper behavior. The genre originated in Old Kingdom Egypt (c. 3050–2190 B.C.E.) as a method of conveying instructions and advice to high officials. *See also* Maat.

women's movement Generally, an activist effort seeking so-cial and political equality for women. English author Mary Wollstonecraft (1759–1797) authored one of the early feminist documents in her 1792 work, *A Vindication of the Rights of Women*. Arguing for educational equality, she opposed policies advocated by Jean-Jacques Rousseau (1712–1778) and other Enlightenment writers, among them traditional roles for men and women. Woman suffrage (the right to vote) emerged as the primary and most crucial objective worldwide since advocates believed that electing their representatives and participating in politics would, in turn, lead to gender equality. By the early twentieth century, the barriers to suffrage fell: Finland gave women the right to vote in 1906, and the United States followed in 1920. After that, the women's movement ebbed and flowed, reemerging as a powerful political force in the 1960s and 1970s, inspired by the writings of Simone de Beauvoir (1908–1986) in the 1950s and Betty Friedan (1921–2006) in the early 1960s. *See also* feminism; suffragists.

workhouses Public institutions in which the able-bodied poor were confined and made to work. Appearing in the mid-seventeenth century as a supplement to religious charity, they were widespread in European cities in the eighteenth and nine-teenth centuries. Implemented to curb rising costs of public welfare, by law, all able-bodied poor were housed together in a kind of dormitory, where they would work to cover any relief they received. Husbands were separated from wives, and al-though not uniformly awful, they were designed to be grim so that the poor would be motivated to seek better jobs that would enable them to leave. Workhouses typically emphasized moral reform and in some cases were a combination of hospital, workshop, and pauper's prison.

working class The term introduced in the early nineteenth century for those who worked in the new factories of the In-dustrial Revolution. The factory system, in which laborers worked together under close supervision, enabled members of this new socioeconomic class to develop a sense of common in-terest and identity.

World Bank An international institution of credit created in the 1940s. With the globalization of finances and of national economies since the 1980s, it has become increasingly power-ful, bolstering the position of wealthy member nations and in-fluencing the domestic policies of smaller countries by refusing to lend them money for armaments. While hailed for having kept the world economy consistent and growing for decades, by the 1990s, the World Bank became the focus of rising fears about globalization. A meeting of the World Bank and International Monetary Fund in 2000 drew protesters, who raised concerns about expanding globalization without seeking more consistent social and economic policies first.

Y

Young Ireland A nationalist movement founded in 1842 by a group of writers seeking to recover Irish history and preserve the Gaelic language, both of which faltered under centuries of English occupation. This movement also sought Irish independence from Britain, with crowds of over 300,000 people turning out at mass meetings in support of breaking away. Though unsuccessful, the movement proved inspirational to later Irish nationalists.

Young Italy An organization founded by Italian journalist Giuseppe Mazzini (1805–1872) in 1831 during his exile to France. Opposed to Austrian rule in northern Italy, Mazzini started this secret society to foment Italian nationalism. He attracted thousands with his message that Italy would touch off a European-wide revolutionary movement, and while his charismatic leadership did concern European conservatives, Mazzini's movement lacked widespread support among the masses and allies in the European power structure. For Mazzini, *young* referred to the age of the Italian nation, which he felt had the potential to become a full-fledged nation in its own right.

Z

zemstvos Regional councils of the Russian nobility established after the emancipation of the serfs in 1861 to deal with education and local welfare issues. The zemstvos became a countervailing force to distant central governments and broadened their vision to include new ways of solving social and economic problems. They were overseen by the gentry, and their decisions could be overridden or ignored by tsarist-appointed local leaders. While the zemstvos served as an attempt to modernize the government, they were ultimately suppressed by the tsar who desired complete autocracy.

ziggurats Large brick temples dominating the Mesopotamian urban landscape after about 3000 B.C.E. They were marked by a stair-step design that dominated the urban landscape and allowed the Sumerian people to gain closer access to their gods.

Zionism A movement that began in the late nineteenth century among European Jews to found a Jewish state. The movement was spearheaded by Theodor Herzl, who started the World Zionist Congress in Basel, Switzerland, in 1897. Adolf Hitler's (1889–1945) attempts to exterminate the Jews during World War II (1939–1945) brought the United States and other Western powers to support the idea of a Jewish state after the war. This goal was realized with the creation of the modern state of Israel in 1948, though not without controversy. To achieve the Jewish state of Israel, the United Nations passed a resolution in 1947 to divide Palestine into an Arab and Jewish state, displacing many Palestinian Arabs. Almost immediately after Israel's formation on May 14, 1948, Lebanon, Syria, Jordan, Egypt, and Iraq invaded it. When the fighting stopped, Israel expanded its borders, but was still not accepted by its Arab neighbors.

Zoroastrianism A religion based on the teachings of the prophet Zarathustra (c. 1200–1000 B.C.E.). Zarathustra proclaimed the deity Ahura Mazda (literally "Wise Lord") to be the "father of Truth," the only god in existence, and the representative of good in an ongoing struggle against evil. Persian kings were Zoroastrians, who believed themselves to be agents of Ahura Mazda on Earth.